MAHARAM'S CURVE

THE EXERCISE HIGH—
HOW TO GET IT,
HOW TO KEEP IT

MAHARAM'S CURVE

THE
EXERCISE
HIGH—
HOW TO
GET IT,
HOW TO
KEEP IT

LEWIS G. MAHARAM, M.D.

W·W·NORTON & COMPANY

NEW YORK   LONDON

First Edition

The text of this book is composed in 11/13 Goudy Old Style
with the display set in Gill Sans Bold and Light
Composition and manufacturing by the Haddon Craftsmen, Inc.
Book design by Margaret M. Wagner.

Library of Congress Cataloging-in-Publication Data
Maharam, Lewis G.
Maharam's curve: The exercise high—how to get it, how to keep it
high / by Lewis G. Maharam, M.D.
p. cm.
Includes index.
1. Exercise. 2. Exercise—Psychological aspects. 3. Health.
I. Title.
GV481.M26 1992
613.7′1—dc20   92-201

ISBN 0-393-03365-1

W.W. Norton & Company, Inc.
500 Fifth Avenue, New York, N.Y. 10110
W.W. Norton & Company Ltd.
10 Coptic Street, London WC1A 1PU

1 2 3 4 5 6 7 8 9 0

To Welabucs . . .
Who Knew . . .

CONTENTS

ACKNOWLEDGMENTS

This book is the result of a lot of research, hard late hours, and liters of Diet Pepsi. There have been many wonderful people giving me constant encouragement and support.

A special thank you to:
my caring literary agent, Joan Raines, who kept things on track.

Many thanks to:
the Norton team—Mary Cunnane, Charlie Flowers, and Donald Lamm—for their time and enthusiasm; Wade Silverman, Ph.D., my friend, colleague, and mentor; the doctors—G. Rankin Cooter, Ph.D., Dr. Murray Gilman, Dr. Allan Levy, and Dr. Andres and Yolanda Rodriguez—for friendship, belief, and input throughout many stages of my work; William Stockton of the *New York Times* who started the early excitement for Maharam's Curve; the Lafayette connection—Dr. Majumdar, who taught me how to do real, true research, and Dr. G. Earl Peace, my best man; dear friends—Alison Hendrie-Judge, Bruce Weddell, and Andrea

and Tom Plate; and last, but not least, my patients who inspire me and are inspired by sports and sports medicine.

Extra thanks to:
my family: Grandmother Bebe, Mother Jane (a remarkable woman), Patsy (number-one in my book) and my adored teammates, Marcia (my light and love) and my Eddy boy.

MAHARAM'S CURVE

THE EXERCISE HIGH—
HOW TO GET IT,
HOW TO KEEP IT

INTRODUCTION

I promise that this book can change your life.

Within weeks, if you follow my revolutionary new program, you will be enjoying exercise—no doubt about it.

If you've always hated to exercise and have finally given up . . . if you are exercising on a regular basis now, but finding it drudgery or painful medicine . . . if you have never started exercising, because you know it would be boring or unpleasant, the facts I've discovered about Maharam's Curve will show you how to attain physical, mental, and emotional pleasure during every workout. Whether you decide to run or swim, work out on a treadmill or do aerobic dance, I've found the key to predictable exercise enjoyment by linking exercise with mood levels. And you will enjoy it!

Why is enjoyment important? Because lack of enjoyment is by far the most common reason people give for not exercising properly; and lack of exercise is responsible for a host of ills in the world population, from mild depression to increased risk of heart disease, from boredom and ennui to decreased sexual interest and debilitating bone disease.

Most people give lip service to the notion that exercise,

like castor oil, is "good for you." Exercise is a bitter pill.
Take my good friend Dr. Andres Rodriguez, medical director of the New York City Marathon. He walks every day,
and hates it. No matter how many marathoners tell him ex-
citedly how much they enjoy running because they've
reached the exhilarating plateau of "runner's high," Andres
is unconvinced. He exercises because he understands the
health benefits, and that knowledge motivates him to stick to
the walking schedule he loathes so much.

Millions of Americans feel the same way, but this book
should change all that.

It is also true, I've found, that some exercisers attain an
"exercise high" but don't recognize it, and therefore can't
retain or recapture it. They might get a pleasant feeling for a
few moments, then feel it dissipate. As I will explain in Chapter Three, one reason that they can't hold on to the quicksil-
ver sensation is because they don't yet understand how and
what they are feeling at any given moment. Also, they probably don't continue exercising at the proper pace to sustain
that mood elevation, or perhaps (which is just as likely in our
highly competitive society) they exercise so strenuously that
they go "past the high."

Follow my explanation of Maharam's Curve and you will
learn to recognize, capture, and repeat that elevated mood.
Certainly, you will never hate exercise again. On the contrary,
as my patients in my sports medicine practice have learned
within a short period of time, it is possible to derive so much
pleasure from exercising that you will be eager to return to
the next exercise session—and the next, and the next.

I have discovered an exercise program that can be adjusted
based upon individual mood, with the aim of making exercise predictably enjoyable.

Everyone has an individual Maharam's Curve, as will
become clear in the first few chapters. You will learn to find
the pattern that emerges from your own exercise experiences. The concept is true whether you exercise regularly

now or have not exercised in years or have never exercised in a planned, systematic way. Even the most experienced, dedicated exercisers have a lot to learn in my program. When I talk later about "getting on the Curve," I mean that you will learn to understand your own Curve and how to take advantage of it so that you will always enjoy exercise. This is something like the importance that Bill Parcells (former New York Giants football head coach) attaches to putting each player in the right position on the playing field to make the play. I am going to put you in the right place for optimum enjoyment of your physical training.

Before I describe Maharam's Curve, let me make clear the perspective from which this book is written. As a physician specializing in sports medicine, which is a relatively new but growing medical discipline, I deal with all of the physical challenges the body faces in exercise. You may have seen a sports medicine physician on TV, sitting on the bench at a pro football game, first-aid kit in hand. That's a role I've played on the field myself, but it's only part of the story. Sports medicine goes back at least to Hippocrates, who treated injured competitors in the ancient Greek Olympic games by using electric eels to apply shock therapy. (This was the first known use of EGS, or electrogalvanic stimulation, which is commonly used by physical therapists today.) Somewhat more recently, in the 1960s, Dr. Kenneth Cooper's landmark book *Aerobics*, a catalyst in this country's ongoing fitness boom, thrust sports medicine into the public limelight as a distinct medical specialty. Even more recently, fellowship training programs have been established to school specialty physicians in this new discipline.

Athletes, of course, think of sports medicine as treatment for broken bones and torn ligaments, and many laypersons assume that I'm an orthopedist, but I'm not. I do pay special attention to skeletal trauma, and I do concentrate on sports-related injuries in my practice, but the basic aim of sports medicine is to provide athletic direction for all people, even those who appear to be in top physical shape. I was fortunate to be among the first generation of physicians to undergo specialty training as a fellow in sports medicine. Therefore, in addition to sports trauma, my concerns include the problems related to rehabilitation, exercise testing and prescription, metabolism, the respiratory and cardiovascular systems, nutrition, internal medicine, obstetrics, gynecology, dermatology, and psychology. Put simply, I am a primary-care physician specializing in sports medicine, and my job is to offer patients a balanced perspective in regard to any injuries or conditions and to continuing programs of physical training.

As some readers will know from experience, the past decade has seen a dramatic change in the relationship of sports medicine to the amateur or weekend athlete. My good friend and pioneer sports medicine physician, Dr. Allan Levy, team physician to the Giants, recalls that when he first went into practice victims of a coronary were kept flat on their backs for six weeks. Afterward, they were allowed to return to work, if it was a sedentary job, and came home every night to sit in a corner, waiting to die. Today, of course, the concept of healing through strengthening is the accepted treatment, for physicians have realized that the heart, like any other muscle, needs to be strengthened in order to work.

In a nutshell, the sports medicine approach to injury is an aggressive rehabilitation that will shorten the disability period and allow the patient to return to normal activity, including an appropriate program of regular exercise. Typically, we do not consider surgery until all other treatment options have failed to work.

Aside from dealing with specific medical problems, my personal goal in my practice is to teach everyone how to maximize life's satisfactions—and indeed prolong them—by exercising properly. Sometimes, with my patients, I have to consider physical limitations and minor injuries as well as improper exercise practices that are counterproductive. You will have to be on the lookout for such potential problems as you read this book.

The focus of this book is on the discovery I made over a period of years and have refined in research and practice: the phenomenon of Maharam's Curve and the radical new promise it brings to everyone—no matter how skilled in training, no matter how resistant to starting—that exercise can be consistently rewarding.

Exhilarating? Sometimes.

Pleasurable? Always.

Here's how I know. . . .

CHAPTER ONE

THE SEARCH

On a blustery, chilly Thanksgiving Day in 1982, huddling
with the other members of the medical team at the 17-mile
mark of the Atlanta Marathon, I kept up my spirits with a
mild joke. As runner after agonized runner came gasping by,
my colleagues and I marveled aloud at the strength of their
internal motivation.

"Yeah, but a good dose of naloxone would stop them
dead in their tracks," I teased.

Not a bad joke, really, since my audience knew that naloxone is a drug that blocks the receptor for endorphins. Their
appreciative laughter didn't suggest I was a threat to the career of Jackie "The Joke Man" Martling, but it did show that
we were all operating under the assumption that the remarkable performances we watched were being fueled by the
body's stress-induced release of pain-killing substances
called endorphins, which I will discuss in further detail in a
moment. We assumed that, with the help of a surge of endorphins caused by their exercise, these struggling human
beings were somehow driving themselves beyond their usual
levels of endurance to complete a grueling, 26-mile course.

They were grimly bearing or ignoring great pain in order to stay in the race.

Not surprisingly, since we were in the midst of our medical studies and fascinated by our growing knowledge of the body, we probably had a bias toward biochemical explanations. In any event, we all agreed. Endorphins kept the athletes going by blocking their pain. The lucky ones, so the theory went, were going to experience a euphoria some people call the "exercise high." Some athletes talk about it as "hitting a rhythm," a phrase that, as you will see, took on special meaning for me. The action of endorphins, in other words, explained why athletes could suddenly reach beyond their normal capacities and ignore pain in order to perform with unusual excellence.

The landmark study that influenced us medical students involved 15 normal volunteer runners—6 women, 9 men— under the supervision of Richard J. Haier, Ph.D., director of psychology at Butler Hospital in Providence, Rhode Island. In 1981, he and his colleagues set out to discover whether strenuous exercise could have an effect on an individual's mood or perception of pain by stimulating the production of endorphins. To establish a baseline of pain, researchers rested a 3-pound weight on a runner's index finger, right at the first joint from the tip, until he or she felt pain. This test was repeated after the subject ran a mile at a self-set pace, then again after a rest of 10 minutes. One day, the runner would be injected with a placebo before running; on another, he or she would receive naloxone, the substance that would block the action of any opiate like endorphins. The sequence of placebo versus naloxone was random in each case, and neither the runners, the physician in attendance, nor the pain tester knew which substance was being given at any time.

Briefly put, the results indicated that runners on placebos took longer to experience pain after their mile-long runs, a strong suggestion that endorphin levels had risen during the exercise period and were decreasing the runner's sensitivity to pain. On the other hand, pain sensitivity was not decreased after exercise when naloxone had been injected, a strong suggestion that naloxone was blocking the beneficial effects of the higher endorphin levels. In sum, Haier and his colleagues surmised that an increased flow of endorphins might be responsible for the elevated mood states reported enthusiastically by some joggers.

This theory seemed so sound, on face value, that I wondered why some scientists did not support it. Right in front of me at the Atlanta Marathon, it seemed, was sufficient proof. Yet I too had doubts, when I considered my own reactions to the so-called "exercise high."

Total Concentration and Awareness

What is the "exercise high"? Does it really exist? What good does it do? Can everyone reach it? What exactly does someone like distance runner Mike Cook mean when describing a "new burst of energy, a renewed interest in what you are doing at that time"?

My answers to these questions began with a completely unexpected revelation in my late teens. Until that magical moment, I had always exercised regularly, but I don't think I ever enjoyed it very much. I liked the feeling of being fit and healthy, but this was the *result* of exercise, not the activity itself. In fact, I was one of those people who took pleasure in the knowledge that I was suffering for a good cause. I threw myself into the required effort. I didn't just like to perspire . . . I loved to sweat.

For a long time, I have been interested in the body's response to the challenges of sports. As a kid, I never missed a sandlot softball game or touch football scramble in the neighborhood. Somehow I knew instinctively that the sensibly exercised body was going to be more successful on the field than the untrained one. The logic in this was obvious. I lived for athletics, and I knew I would have more fun on the field if I stayed in shape. Then in the seventh grade came the disturbing discovery that I had Achilles tendinitis. No longer capable of competing in group sports, I had to find an exercise that would be challenging to my body and enjoyable as well.

For me, swimming proved to be the answer. By my teens, I was swimming 6 to 8 miles a week. When I wasn't in school, I was in the local health-club pool. There was an important psychological plus, as would become apparent to me when I discovered Maharam's Curve. Because I was growing up in the relatively severe winters of New York's Long Island, I must have associated the pleasant sensations of swimming with the seemingly endless warm summers of childhood. Perhaps more to the point, my family escaped with relative frequency to Miami Beach during the northern cold months. My grandparents lived there in the sort of high-rise that is fairly common in Florida; however, to a New York boy starved for warmth and sunlight their apartment's pool was paradise—even if my lips turned blue before my parents could convince me to leave the cooling waters late in the day. Like my own five-year-old son today, I wanted to stay in the water forever. But that was not the high I was to experience later on, when I first began to sense the truth about the relationship between exercise and feelings of well-being.

Instead, the peak of good feeling on Maharam's Curve is a combination of psychological and physical factors coming together to produce an optimum mood that is sustainable. That moment is immediately recognizable the first time you experience it, as I would learn in my teens; and it is different for each person, a corollary I would not understand until much later. My discoveries began to take shape, not coincidentally, in a swimming pool at summer camp.

The First Time

The conditions at Rolling Hills Day Camp in Nassau County, New York, in 1971 could hardly have been less promising for any kind of positive life-changing experience, because I was under tremendous psychological pressure at the time. At 16, I was the youngest candidate ever to apply for the position of pool director at Rolling Hills, then a very swanky and highly competitive day camp. To get the job, I would have to pass the tough Nassau County Life Guard Test within six days. The test included speed and distance swims, a long and demanding haul even for athletic young-sters in tip-top shape. Even worse, we had to "rescue" a 6-foot, 3-inch, 250-pound "drowning victim" who struggled violently to break our cross-chest carry as soon as we began pulling him back to safety. The whole challenge was daunt-ing for a 16-year-old. Indeed, it was unusual for someone so young even to be considered a candidate, but the former pool director had been summarily fired and a replacement was needed quickly. The staff knew my potential, for I had been going to the camp from childhood on. But no one was going to do me any favors. I had to train in cram-course style after a full day's work as a swim counselor at the camp. Lap after lap in the camp's outdoor, Olympic-sized pool on chilly, fog-bound evenings in early summer, the water felt like melted ice.

One particular evening, I was long past my second wind and giving in to exhaustion. Breathing was an effort, and my leg muscles ached terribly. I was torturing myself for a good cause, much the way my friend Andres forces himself to do his hated walking. It had to be done, and so I did it.

By chance, a girl named Janice, leader of the older girls' synchronized swimming team I was teaching, decided to play her practice record through the pool loudspeaker. Suddenly, the voice of Maureen McGovern rang out in the chill and damp of the night. Instantly, I was swimming in time with the beat of the music. The words "there has got to be a morning after" were like a strong wind at a runner's back, the kind of gust that almost lifts someone off the ground. The words gave me wings.

I wasn't swimming any longer; excuse the pun, but I was "floating"—feeling as if I could swim forever, all tiredness completely gone.

What was this amazing sensation? The next night, I went back to the pool with a plan in mind. I did some warm-up laps for about ten minutes, just as I ordinarily did. Next, a little nervously, I put on the record and dived back into the pool. The music filled the night and sank deep inside me as well.

And the music did it again. I began to swim almost effortlessly. I felt light as a feather and found myself stroking the water with remarkable ease of movement and speed. Clearly, I had stumbled upon an exercise pace that specifically gave me, Lewis Maharam, the high. The way that particular song just happened to set a specific *pace* got me to my peak. To recapture that pace, I wouldn't need the recording again. I could just imagine the song and start swimming in sync with the beat. From then on, I looked forward every day to my training, and I passed that lifeguard test like a dolphin.

Does It Work for Everyone?

This peak experience at a stressful moment during my teen years was unforgettable and strangely intriguing—so much so that it helped set me down the path I would follow in my life's work as a sports medicine physician. Without really thinking about the medical implications, I pondered over the possible explanations for my amazing high. Basically, I wanted to know why some people achieved this high rather often and others never did. I wondered if there was a relationship between success in sports and the high. And what about successful professional athletes? Perhaps each one of them found an optimum exercise pace intuitively and therefore always enjoyed their training.

My first attempts to share my discovery were less than wildly successful. Naturally, I couldn't wait to tell all of my friends at camp. They swam as I had, pacing themselves to the McGovern record . . . and felt nothing. But, even though no one had an experience like mine, a few said that they had felt such sensations before, swimming at their own pace. At the time, I was disappointed and puzzled. Now, looking back after discovering the theory of Maharam's Curve, I realize that I had missed the critically important factor of individualized pace.

I didn't give up, though, because I wanted to learn how to share my discovery with all exercisers, whether champion athlete or 20-mile-a-week jogger. Achieving that elevated state is so pleasurable, such a fundamentally natural exhilaration of mind and body, that I consider it one of life's joys. (Most runners agree, for they often compare notes about their experiences of runner's high.)

Years later, champion U.S. swimmer John Naber would tell me that his own exercise high was "no pain . . . total concentration and awareness." The great Wimbledon tennis champion Arthur Ashe would write me that his high occurs when the "body feels in sync with nature" and he feels an "absence of conscious thought, a sense of timelessness, an absence of stress." Joan Van Ark, the well-known actress on TV's "Knots Landing," talks enthusiastically about being "in total sync with your body, everything moving as one unit."

The University of Chicago's Mihaly Caikszentmihalyi, a professor of psychology and education, speaks of it as "flow" and pictures time standing still as an athlete (or painter or opera singer, for that matter) concentrates so totally that he becomes completely absorbed in his activity. Each movement seems to flow from thought and intent, without effort. Mind and body, aim and effect, are in perfect harmony.

I have written this book because I want everyone to feel the distinctive euphoria that comes at the peak of aerobic performance, just as I tried to encourage my fellow campers back at Rolling Hills. But I now know, as a sports physician, that the effort of regular exercise can be daunting. At first it seems boring, or impossible. In fact, probably four out of five Americans who start an exercise program in adult life will give up after only two weeks. Yet we all know that regular exercise is essential to good health. Maharam's Curve can help everyone continue to exercise.

Perhaps it will help you understand how the Curve works if I give more background about my slowly developing grasp of the concept over the years.

The Endorphin Myth

In medical school I could concentrate on the technical aspects of the problem. Before I was able to discover the whole truth about Maharam's Curve, I had to deal with the assumption I had shared with my fellow med students on that brisk Thanksgiving Day in Atlanta—the myth of endorphins. Commonly believed by many athletes over the past couple of decades, and widely popularized in a stream of newspaper and magazine articles, the theory ran that the feeling of being "in the zone" is a physiological reaction caused by maximal exercise. (This was the popular version of the theory investigated by Haier and his colleagues in the placebo versus naloxone study I mentioned earlier.)

It was known that strenuous exertion stimulates the body to release morphine-like substances known as endorphins directly into the bloodstream. Suppose these endorphins also began circulating through the brain as a response to physical stress . . . and there's the answer: psychological euphoria occurs because the exerciser's exertions have caused the brain to comfort itself with a quick fix of endorphins. Punish the body; the mind takes away the pain.

To many, this theory is still attractive, but it has one very inconvenient characteristic. It can't be proven, because of a characteristic of the body known as the "blood-brain barrier." Many substances, including endorphins, cannot cross this barrier between the bloodstream in the body and the blood vessels in the brain, or vice versa. This protective device helps ensure that brain-damaging substances don't get into the brain; it also maintains the balance of the chemicals the brain needs. (You know more about this phenomenon than you may think: your doctor doesn't prescribe certain antibiotics for certain diseases, because their molecules are too large to pass the blood-brain barrier, but the molecules of alcohol you drink are small enough to get through with no problem.) Because of the blood-brain barrier, therefore, a test of the bloodstream will not directly show whether or not the substance has actually passed over into or out of the brain itself, thus having a direct effect upon mood.

Some researchers assume that the appearance of endorphins in the bloodstream, known as peripheral endorphins, makes a case for the parallel appearance of endorphins in our brains. In my view, the case hasn't been made strongly enough, even though it has been arguably bolstered by the discovery of endorphins in the brains of laboratory rats. In these experiments, the rats were killed immediately after they experienced physical stress in running on treadmills. When their brains were quickly removed and run through blenders, tests showed that significant amounts of endorphins were present. By extrapolation, some researchers have surmised that physical stress in humans must also produce endorphins in the human brain. Even if that extrapolation holds some truth, however, endorphins would be only one factor in the confluence of variables that produces the exercise high.

The exercise high has been linked with two specific phenomena. The first one, which can be reached within weeks by following my suggested program, is a consistently attainable elevation of mood. This is the feeling that most athletes talk about, if they are aware of an exercise-induced feeling of emotional and mental well-being.

The second, and rarer, exercise high is a virtual "explosion" of good feeling. As I will explain in more detail later in the book, not everyone experiences this special feeling, and you should not make it the goal of your exercise program. If it happens, it is a wonderful bonus, and you will certainly recognize it instantly. The first type of high, however, is consistently satisfying, even exhilarating, and will be the emotional spark to keep you exercising.

An Addiction?

In some popular writing, the use of the image of the high leads to talk of addiction, and I've drawn upon that idea briefly. But exercise does not have the down sides of true addiction. True, the imagery of drugged states can be helpful in describing the high. I certainly know what Burt Grossman of the San Diego Chargers means by saying that his exercise high makes him feel "in a cloud." But it does not follow that the high, like a drug-induced euphoria, comes crashing down. Definitely, it does not lead to the common symptoms of physical withdrawal, like vomiting, muscle twitching, nausea, runny nose, diarrhea, profuse sweating, and elevated body temperature and heart rate. Instead, at worst, withdrawal from the exercise high is a matter of increased frustration and bad temper. One of my patients, a hard-working lawyer who has learned to reach his exercise high with some consistency, occasionally becomes too deeply involved in an important case to keep training regularly. I know, because his private secretary calls me soon afterward to plead, "Get my boss running again!" After a few days of concentrated work and no exercise, he starts throwing things around the office, knocking over stacks of papers, and yelling at everyone in sight. When we urge him back into running regularly, he's congenial again.

Dr. Levy had a similar experience some years ago, he tells me, with Dave Jennings, who was then All-Pro Punter for the New York Jets:

Dave was not only a great punter, he was an all-around top athlete who excelled in basketball and usually ran as a receiver on the "opposing team" in practice. His physical workouts were almost staggering, but he totally enjoyed them. Typically, Dave was upbeat, an extremely bright person with a wild sense of humor.

Twice in his career when I saw Dave injured, however, I also witnessed a remarkable personality change when he was unable to continue working out during his recovery. Overnight, he was unhappy and also impatient with himself and his condition. "Chatterbox" Dave became almost morose. This was obviously a clear picture of someone who had lost the good feeling of his own personal exercise high.

As Dr. Levy has also said, "Those of us who spend full time dealing with athletes at all levels have also been aware of individuals who need to exercise to maintain their feelings of well-being."

In my own experience, I found that regular exercise could produce a kind of "psychological addiction," if the term is not too strong or misleading. When I was first thinking about the sources of exercise pleasure, and a couple of days had passed after I had had a good workout, I invariably found myself wanting to be back in the pool.

I missed the high. I wanted to sustain my good moods.

In the next chapter, you'll see how my curiosity about my own intensely personal experiences led to a revelation about the biological and mental factors that produce Maharam's Curve.

CHAPTER TWO

HOW IT CAME TOGETHER

> The secret to a long life and years of
> running is to make running a pleasure and
> pleasure your running.
>
> —Joe Henderson,
> *Runner's World*

The idea of doing serious research on the exercise phenomenon came when I was in my second year of medical school at Emory University in Atlanta. By then I had learned that runners especially are prone to become "exercise junkies." Do endorphins make them run longer? This was the question, long pondered casually, that occurred to me so vividly that Thanksgiving Day at the running of the Atlanta Marathon.

No one else had this concern on the front burner, but I began cajoling and conspiring around the Atlanta university community. Soon I had some very fine allies: G. Rankin Cooter, Ph.D., at Georgia State University's Exercise Physiology Lab, and Dr. Murray Gilman, of Emory University's Pulmonary Department. Over the course of two years, my research would reveal some unexpected answers.

At GSU's lab, I brought together a select group of unusually fit male athletes, mean age 31. In choosing these subjects, I looked for nearly identical physical condition, similar patterns of regular exercise, and apparently the same level of endurance. I chose only men in a further effort to have as few variables as possible in this controlled study. If women had been included, each would have had to be at the same specific point in the menstrual cycle, because hormonal factors may or may not be involved in the body's release of endorphins.

The design of the project was simplicity itself. On three occasions over a two-week period, each participant performed a maximal treadmill exercise test. To establish a "control" as baseline, the athlete was asked to perform until he felt drained and exhausted. On all three tests, the athlete was asked to continue running past the point of perceived exhaustion, while we cheered him on like cheerleaders at a basketball game.

Just before the second and third tests, each subject was given either 1 cc of a placebo (in this case, the sterile salt water known as saline) or naloxone. The choices were random, made without my knowledge. In other words, this was a double-blind study, since neither I nor the athletes knew what was being administered. Only Dr. Gilman knew and recorded which substance each runner was given before each test. If Athlete A was given the placebo on the second test, he would be given naloxone on the third, or vice versa. The saline, of course, could have no physiological effect. As for the naloxone, I didn't really expect the athlete to be "stopped dead in his tracks," but he would at least feel the pain that the body might offer in response to the stress of the treadmill test. You can picture this process by imagining a key inserted into a lock and turned. The endorphin key turns the cell's receptor lock, releasing a flow of pleasurable sensations within the cell. The naloxone (a competitive inhibitor) jams the lock, in a sense, preventing the cascade of reactions within a cell that is the pleasure-giving, pain-masking endorphin response.

After all the results were tabulated and analyzed, Dr. Gilman informed me whether each athlete was given naloxone in the second or the third test.

During all of these performance trials, my GSU colleagues and I kept close watch on a range of changing physical factors: maximal heartbeat rate, cardiorespiratory parameters, endorphin levels in the bloodstream, and time on the treadmill. For accurate measuring of these peripheral endorphin levels, we relied upon blood samples analyzed by the Yerkes Institute. We also kept a record of oxygen consumption and carbon dioxide levels. Experienced exercisers will probably recognize the standard measure of oxygen consumption as $\dot{V}O_2$ max, which indicates the amount of oxygen consumed and therefore is a measure of fitness.

While we analyzed the physical picture, we also assessed the athletes' feelings during each session as they ran. Before, during, and after the exercise they were given a "mood scale." This standard psychological tool was to become basic to Maharam's Curve and will be explained in detail later. (Some readers will recognize that the scale is a slight modification of Lasagna's 1955 scale.) For now, it is worth noting that the scale is a well-accepted, efficient, accurate, simple-to-use gauge of an individual's overall mood state at any given moment.

As I've already hinted, I was in for a surprise. My previous assumptions about endorphins had inspired a theory—that the runners would run farther—which in turn helped me design a research project, which in turn . . . disproved my original theory!

For the data would prove convincingly that the athletes ran just as far with saline as with endorphin-blocking naloxone. And their mood levels reached the same peak, the same kind of runner's high, under both conditions. In other words, the level of endorphins in the bloodstream did not correlate with either mood or physical endurance, where these highly motivated, superbly fit athletes were concerned.

Their exercise high was essentially a subjective experience. The key was psychological. Whatever the purpose of endorphin production under physical stress, it is not necessary to keep runners running, running farther, and running happily. I had to look for some other explanation.

Our results would shatter the myth of a one-to-one relationship between mood elevation during exercise and endorphin levels. At the same time, like all good research, the Maharam Project would raise more questions than it answered. What role is played by endorphins in the body?

On the other hand, as I will explain, I learned about the existence of Maharam's Curve, and I found that you could accurately assess mood during any exercise session.

Remember, I had approached this study with the assumption, held by many athletes and researchers, that the physical stress of exercise stimulates the production of endorphins, and those endorphins alone produce the pleasurable feelings that make exercise enjoyable.

But that wasn't it. There were other factors involved, but what were they? Were they all equally significant? How did they interrelate with each other? And, most important, could they be easily understood and managed so that anyone could learn to attain his or her own mood-enhancing exercise rhythm?

What Did It All Mean?

Fortunately, the participants in my project were able to add information and insights of their own that would lead me nearer to understanding the constellation of factors that work together to produce the exercise high.

Interviews with these dedicated runners revealed a kind of "runner's golden mean" for optimum mood state. (These runners were all the same in terms of general physical condition and VO_2 max.) In other words, the men who regularly ran either quite a lot—say, 52 miles a week—or as little as 15 miles a week did not have mood profiles that were as elevated or high as those of the athletes who ran *in the middle range* of about 24 miles.

All of the data agreed. Neither exhaustive nor minimal exercise improved the runner's mood. Vigorous exercise at the appropriate level, however, was always beneficial for mood enhancement. Runners at this level, it turned out, were the ones likely to experience a runner's high on a regular basis. They found their own personal best rhythm. They were having a hell of a good time. The runners who did too much or too little were just going through the motions.

These were tremendously exciting discoveries. The project had not only disproved the supposed one-to-one linkage between exercise highs and blood endorphin levels, it had also revealed that the actual linkage is at least partly psychological. Further, I had learned that the specific amount of exercise is important in attaining the exercise peak on a regular basis. And it was the pace (as I had discovered for myself by exercising to the rhythm of a song) that dependably got these runners to their peaks.

Finally, I was beginning to see that the performance of my best runners was very much like the work of the great athletes I had admired since childhood. Champions, it seemed to me, almost always have a similar "addiction" to training and exercise. Are they able to sense the combination of physical and mental factors that will produce their individual highs?

Long-distance runners and other endurance athletes, in particular, are simply unable to forgo exercise. In magazine profiles and other published interviews, professional athletes and dedicated amateurs generally make clear that idleness drives them up the wall. Injured players, forced to stay idle in order to recuperate, tend to be a miserable lot, just as Dr. Levy learned with Dave Jennings.

"Look within," says the philosopher, and so I did. Ever

since that first experience in the pool at the Rolling Hills Day Camp, I was conscious that regular exercise elevated my mood. The reverse, if I was honest about it, was also true. A week without a strenuous workout could darken my internal horizons. Two weeks and I was ready to chew radiators.

In putting my project data together with my own experiences, I was determined to come up with a program that could make anyone enjoy exercise so much that it would become a regular part of a normally healthy and happy life. My program would have to be clear, workable, and immediately rewarding. For the experienced exerciser, this program had to offer a dramatic new method of getting the optimum physical and psychological benefits at every workout. But it also had to give the unpracticed, wary new exerciser a taste of the rewards of serious exercise as quickly as possible. Six weeks, based upon my experience observing people who had never exercised before, seemed to be about the maximum that nonexercisers would invest in an exercise program before giving up.

Meanwhile, I had turned to that most enthusiastic of research assistants, the computer. From the physiological and psychological data assembled during my project with the ten near-identical athletes, the computer printouts showed a pattern appearing again and again. It rang true, without exception, for each of the ten runners in my project. I have continued to find this pattern over the years in interviews with other athletes.

The simple, bell-shaped curve shown on page 36 is the basis of this book. Throughout the next few chapters, I will be returning to the basic pattern of Maharam's Curve in order to refine the complete picture of the relationship I discovered between mood level and exercise programs. As William Stockton, a *New York Times* reporter phrased it in an article about my original research, my discovery is indeed a "powerful idea." (It was Stockton, in fact, who coined the term "Maharam's Curve.") The power in the idea is the rev-

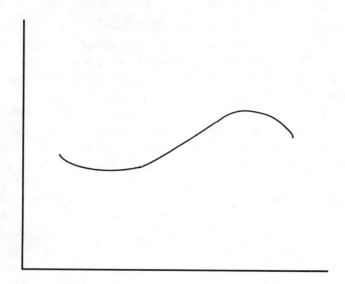

olutionary linkage between exercise and mood. It has never been done before. The concept central to Maharam's Curve is simple, which is part of its power, but strong enough to challenge long-standing misconceptions about exercise. Since my program brings together many different aspects of exercise and can guarantee that anyone will enjoy exercise once the linked concepts are grasped, this idea is likely to change the way most people practice exercise.

Powerful as this idea is, however, the essential facts can be quickly grasped. The scale up the left margin charts the exerciser's mood state. The higher the curve, the more euphoric the mood. The scale along the bottom of the graph charts a series of exercise sessions, each one using the same pace (e.g., number of minutes per mile) but varying levels of exertion (e.g., number of miles actually run that day). In this simple example, you can see several points along one exerciser's curve, each one representing the mood level reached by a runner during one of his exercise sessions.

Although his running pace was maintained at the same level in each workout, the results varied dramatically. In one session, for example, he reached his psychological peak (the top of the curve) after running a strenuous six miles. Note that the basic shape of this runner's curve is universal for all exercisers; it is a global curve. Different exercisers will attain their peaks at differing points on the scale, however; in other words, the entire curve will be moved to one side or the other on the scale, as if a roller-coaster track is being trucked sideways without losing its basic shape.

Maharam's Curve is a startling discovery. For each of my ten male subjects, I was able to plot an exercise curve that predicted an optimum exercise level. It was unique to the individual, incorporating his own reactions on the mood scale and the physiological data I had recorded during the three treadmill tests. Keying his activity to this curve, the runner could learn how much exercise was necessary to reach his high.

The discovery has wide implications. Why couldn't everyone learn to discover and understand their own individual curve? No reason at all. Everyone could. My subsequent work has shown that this method can help anyone, no matter how unskilled or untrained, reach the peak of exercise enjoyment at every workout.

That is the message of this book: a powerful new way of exercising that is as rewarding psychologically as it is physically. Because your exercise program will be adjusted according to your mood levels, Maharam's Curve will help your body enhance its natural drive to exercise regularly. You will discover reserves of energy that you never suspected you could draw upon. By following the curve, you will learn to use exercise to manipulate your mood level. In short, Maharam's Curve will get you in shape by teaching you how to get a predictable exercise high . . . and you are going to feel happier, more energetic, sexier, more confident, and younger every day for the rest of your exercising life.

This is the essence of the relationship Maharam's Curve provides between exercise and mood: Because you will learn to enjoy exercise, you will get in shape, as the natural by-product of your exercise; and because you will be in shape, you will be that much happier with yourself *and healthier*. Exercise, which becomes fun, produces fitness, which makes you feel better physically and emotionally. That's the promise of Maharam's Curve.

Before I talk about the actual work of learning and adhering to Maharam's Curve, it's important to deal with a potential attitude problem. If you already exercise regularly, you don't have to worry about this. But, for those who are just starting, let's recall that four out of five people who begin an exercise program without adequate physical and mental preparation are likely to lose interest and give up. I'm acutely aware of this obstacle. With my patients, of course, I have the advantage of looking them straight in the eye and promising, "This will work!" Weekly office appointments reinforce that message. When there's a problem, we work together to fine-tune the individual exercise program. I'd like my patients to think of me as the mechanic for Maharam's Curve, if that notion helps.

But without meeting with you directly, how can I help you sustain faith in Maharam's Curve for the weeks before it finally kicks in for you?

Nancy Ditz, who has twice won the Los Angeles Marathon, suggests that you involve someone else. "Find a partner who shares your goals and articulate *your* goals to that person and others," she says. "You are less likely to give up if others are in your corner."

Good advice. But the most important person in your corner, of course, is you. In the next chapter, I talk about the essential matter of motivation.

CHAPTER THREE

MOTIVATION

It is very easy to understand the basic concept of Maharam's Curve. Making it work effectively for you the individual, however, is going to require a sensible amount of mental work. With the patients in my sports medicine practice, my usual first step is to encourage an increase in self-awareness. This is a specific aim, not a vague New Age wandering about in the backstairs of the brain. I want them to understand the practical concept many successful professional athletes have learned for themselves, or just sensed: mind and body have to work together.

Let's talk for a moment about motivation. You won't successfully grasp Maharam's Curve until you learn how to listen to the constant, and constantly changing, flow of messages from your mind and your body. Motivation is the tool I use to help my patients start to understand their mood, to recognize their true motives for wanting to start exercising. (As you will see in this chapter, that's not quite as easy as it sounds.) Motivation will help you learn to assess your own emotional state at specific moments. You will use this height-

ened self-awareness to plan the program of exercise that max-
imizes your own personal exercise high.

The specific nature of an individual's motivation is not
critical to my work, since I am not a psychologist, but motivation, when properly understood, is the key to beginning to
use the all-important mood scale. It is a technique of learning
to identify the subtle mood changes (and subtle they will be)
that occur as you train. Learning the technique takes practice. It will also take concentrating on tuning in accurately to
your constantly changing mood states.

Let me repeat: recognizing your mood at a given moment
is essential to discovering your own personal Curve, and if
you resist this attempt at understanding, you will not get to
your optimum mood levels with any reliability.

I have found that patients who come to me about starting
an exercise program rarely recognize their true motives at
our first meeting. They think they do, but, generally speaking, they fall back on some conventional explanation rather
than taking a careful look at the reasons they really want to
change their lives.

Since many people simply cannot find their own Curve
without attempting to understand their motivation, I always
listen closely to any new patient, hoping to sense the truth
beneath the automatic or ill-considered response. In a manner of speaking, they need to be in the mood to get the
mood. Much of the time, I find myself blurting out a line so
useful it's become almost my trademark: "No, that's not it."

How Some of My Patients See It

When Crystal E., a 35-year-old self-described "house-
wife," breezed into my office, other patients in the waiting
room could not resist exchanging raised eyebrows and wry
glances. Early on a weekday morning, a mild spring day, she
was swathed in dyed mink. Underneath, she was wearing a

trendy, blue leather dress and remarkably high heels. Her very pretty face was artfully made up, her hair stylishly tousled, her fingernails beautifully manicured.

But Mrs. E. was no mere clotheshorse without personality. She knew what she wanted. Abruptly, confidently, she explained that she had heard I could "make people enjoy exercise." She had tried a workout or two every now and then but had always been bored by the whole thing. How could I help?

I answered her question with a question: Why did she suddenly want to start exercising? She blithely gave one of the standard responses: "Sounds like a fun idea."

"No," I said. "That's not it."

Normally self-assured, Crystal E. was taken aback for a moment, but she got the point. As I explained to her, I was not borrowing a psychoanalyst's hat, but "I'm using a tool to help you understand your feelings." As I often do, I asked her to go home and think about her real motives. Get in touch with her feelings. (If a cliché works, more power to it!) I suggested she write down, if she thought it would help, the thoughts that came to mind when she thought about initiating this change in her behavior patterns.

A week later, Mrs. E.'s re-entrance was no less arresting, but her approach to my program had deepened and matured, because of her own serious consideration of her aims.

"My looks are very important to me," she said straight out. "To who I am, to what I think about myself. To tell the truth, Doctor, I'm afraid. I'm thirty-five and I see other women my age getting old and flabby. I'm terrified of that. I don't want plastic surgery. I have never liked exercise, but I have decided I have to do it. I need you to help me like it. I need you to help me do it."

"Yes," I said. "That's it. You've done a remarkable job of uncovering your real motives."

Not surprisingly, this self-aware patient would "get on the Curve" (discover and understand how to control her own

Curve) faster than almost anyone else who's ever come to me. Within two weeks of trying my program, she was experiencing mood elevation at every workout. She was highly motivated and, equally important, she had started to become introspective and was ready for the next step, the mood cards. (On a lighter note, it turned out that a minor stumbling block was her fear of looking unattractive when she worked out in the company of other people. I informed her about Gucci exercise outfits, and her fear vanished. Clearly, I had shown her the way to new horizons.)

Mrs. E. was also afraid that she might look unfeminine—"like a sweathog," as she put it—if she exercised too frequently. Many women share such fears, despite all of the hype about working out, and I always show them a statement by Florence Griffith Joyner, who is physically amazing in every way: "I am a pioneer, and sports is my frontier. It's been hard for a woman to be strong, fast, *and* feminine, but that's changing. I'm muscular, but that strength and endurance enhances, not diminishes, my femininity. I can wear six-inch nails and one-legged bodysuits and set world records. And leave a lot of men in the dust."

A very different type of patient, a no-nonsense 36-year-old emergency-room nurse with a slight weight problem, was just as unaware of her real motives at our first meeting.

Jessie R. came straight to the point. As a professional, she was well informed about the dangers of a high cholesterol count. According to some recent research she'd read, regular exercise could help the problem. Never in her life had she found time or inclination for regular workouts. That was something, as far as she knew, that air-headed jocks did for mysterious reasons of their own. The cholesterol connection had changed her mind. She had come to me because she knew that I could help her design a program that would specifically be addressed to lowering her blood cholesterol levels.

With her steady, blue-eyed gaze, Ms. R. spoke logically.

She had her facts organized. Her businesslike manner and plain cotton dress suggested that she knew exactly what she was doing.

I considered her explanation for a few moments.

"No," I said finally. "That's not really it."

She was not amused. Some nurses feel that physicians don't always respect them as fellow professionals, but I hastened to make my feelings clear on that score. (One of the little-known but tremendously significant stories of contemporary medical practice, by the way, is the increasing level of responsibility sought by nurses. Perhaps a few traditional physicians have resisted this trend, but most of us welcome the greater sharing that now characterizes patient care. Nurses and physicians work more effectively as members of a cooperative team, and the patient benefits.) Ms. R. has the kind of job where she spends most of her waking hours worrying about others and she grudgingly agreed that she'd been too busy to sit down and closely examine her personal feelings. She understood the importance of getting it right.

A week later, a bemused, thoughtful Jessie R. walked into my office. "Well, Doctor, I really did need that extra time to think. I wasn't facing my real motivation last week, but now I know." Quite recently, she explained, her father had suffered an abdominal aortic aneurysm, a life-threatening condition that had required surgery and a long convalescence. All things being equal, he was now likely to live for years, for the surgical procedure proved effective. During the actual operation, however, the family suffered terribly, aware that he was in a frighteningly iffy situation because of the seriousness of his condition. Ms. R.'s father could have died during or soon after the procedure, but he was lucky. As she understood, the medical problem is likely to run in families; moreover, it is probably exacerbated by sedentary habits. She was so terrified of having the same experience as her father that, at the conscious level, she had not been able to face and deal with her feelings. "I don't want to go through what he did and does," she said. "That's why I want to learn how to exercise regularly."

"You seem sure of yourself now," I said. "You're starting to be able to understand your feelings."

In neither of these cases, nor in any other in my practice, was I able to intuit the motivation for a patient. We all have to find the answer for ourselves. I was simply able to guess, after some years in this practice, that a standard-issue explanation did not adequately express the inner feelings of the unique individual sitting across from my desk. And I used my surmise as a tool to encourage that individual to uncover something deeper at work.

What About You?

Now, it's time to start the process for yourself.

As a unique individual, you should start the process by taking the time to consider your own motives for picking up this book and deciding to start an exercise program or deciding to try to get more pleasure out of the exercising you already do. Write those motives down on a piece of paper or file card. Then imagine me asking if those are *really* your reasons for wanting to exercise.

Look again at those apparent motives.

Are they written the way you would naturally say them, or do they sound like the kind of half-true slogans we all pick up from TV or from reading? What do they have to do with what you really want out of life, with what you think you're missing? You may think you don't need to think about these questions, but I disagree—and experience in the office is on my side. Somehow, we all tend to forget what is really important to us. Without knowing the true answers, we can't start making the changes that will help us earn what we want.

Keep this piece of paper or file card. As you read more about Maharam's Curve in this book, you will be testing the validity of these motives in the back of your mind. In a week or so, just like the patients who come to my office for a personalized program, you should return to your written statements. Do they still make sense? Are they only part of the story? The effectiveness of Maharam's Curve will depend a great deal on your determination to start off honestly and assess your motives frankly. Since we are dealing with mind as well as matter, the mind has to be as clearly focused and in tune as possible.

Living Longer?

You may be one of those who really does understand your personal motivation to exercise. I certainly don't mean to suggest that you should go overboard and distrust a rationale that feels profoundly right to you, once you've taken some time to focus on it.

Thurston G., for example, a 45-year-old white-collar worker, understood his motivation perfectly when he came to me. With tears welling in his eyes, he explained that both of his parents had died of heart attacks when they were only in their fifties. Now his children were in elementary school, his wife and he both loved their jobs, he had plans for a long, full, active life. He was terrified at the likelihood that he faced a genetically ordained death sentence in ten years or less. He wanted an exercise program that would lower his blood cholesterol level and help him lose weight. He wanted, as the bottom line, a program that would help him live longer.

Yes, that *was* it. No doubt about it this time. He was firmly in touch with his motivation.

Perhaps surprisingly to some readers, his expectations about increased longevity were not at all unrealistic. Hippocrates, "father of medicine," knew as much 24 centuries ago. "All parts of the body that have a function," he wrote, "if used in moderation and exercised in labors in which each is accustomed, become thereby healthy, well-developed, and age more slowly, but if unused and left idle they become liable to disease, defective in growth, and age quickly."

My wise friend, Dr. Ira Schulman, a cardiologist, has explained the concept with an up-to-date analogy. If you have a classic, 1957 Thunderbird with a worn-out motor, you can get a smoother ride by changing the oil, repairing the transmission, and putting in new shock absorbers. In other words, you reduce the demands upon the wheezing engine, allowing it to function more efficiently. The engine will, in a sense, live longer. If an aging body's engine is the heart, exercise helps it function more efficiently by toning up other muscles and increasing the consumption of oxygen required to keep the body working normally. And the heart, a muscle itself, also gets trained. The demands upon the engine of the body, or heart muscle, are thus decreased; the heart lasts longer because it has to work less on a daily basis.

With aging, men and women alike tend to lose some bone mass, although women are more prone to the bone-degenerating disease known as osteoporosis. Research has shown persuasively that regular exercise can stimulate an increase in bone mass. By age 60, most people have lost about 30 percent of their original muscle power, but exercise training reduces the percentage of breakdown by helping to keep muscle tissue and fibers firm and strong.

Chest walls that surround the lungs will stiffen with age and the surrounding muscles will weaken, causing shortness of breath. (The lungs remain strong, but they lose the surrounding support.) Exercise increases the flexibility of the chest walls and strengthens the respiratory muscles, as it also helps prevent the age-related stiffening of joints, ligaments, and tendons throughout the body.

Finally, it has been proved that physical activity improves mental alertness in aging. Louise Clarkson-Smith of Scripps College compared men and women who exercise at least 75 minutes a week with those who exercise less than 10 minutes weekly. She discovered that the heavy exercisers had better memories, more accurate powers of reasoning, and quicker reactions.

For all of these reasons, then, Mr. G. was quite right to turn to exercise as a way of slowing the aging process. Because of his strong personal motivation, he was so accurately focused that he eagerly cooperated with some nutritional recommendations I made. With similar enthusiasm, he fairly leaped upon Maharam's Curve and his program went like clockwork. He is a very happy man today.

If you know your motives as well as he did, you have taken an important first step toward mastering the technique of Maharam's Curve.

Next you have to use your newfound insight to assess your changing moods.

LEARNING YOURSELF— THE MOOD SCALE

> Ninety percent of sports is mental; the
> other half is in your head.
>
> —Yogi Berra

Why do we have to learn to recognize and assess our mood changes? Aren't most of us aware of our feelings at any given moment?

Actually, it is the rare individual who characteristically knows exactly how she is feeling—and why—if you ask her without warning to describe her mood.

Most of the time, we all go through our busy days without stopping to pay close attention to the melange of conflicting feelings we experience. We put our mild depression out of mind while we work, or we discount our anxiety, hoping it will go away. Even when we're feeling happy, we don't usually give in to our joy in public places by letting out a whoop.

How do you feel right now, as you read this book?

"Nothing special." Nothing special? You are a thinking, feeling, acting adult smack in the midst of your life on Earth, and you aren't feeling anything special? More likely you are not focusing on your mood of the moment, which is probably a complex combination of reactions to the many stresses, victories, pleasures, and pains of the past few hours or days.

It is important to understand the role played by the next

step explained in this chapter: Maharam's Curve will not work for you until you learn to take your emotional temperature at the flick of a mood-scale card. In fact, as you have no doubt already noticed, a set of ten detachable cards has been bound in the signature of this book. These are essential day-to-day tools for monitoring and refining your exercise program. Now that you have used the tool of assessing your motivation for exercise, the real work begins: assessing your mood. The cards will become your guideposts to developing your own personal pathway along Maharam's Curve. If you have not already done so, gently detach them now and spread them out in front of you.

You will be using these mood-scale cards several times a day, so treat them well. These are not just a device to help you understand the concepts in this book; they are working tools that will be central to your ongoing involvement in Maharam's Curve.

These cards are based upon the same mood scale I used in my experiments at the Georgia State University laboratory. Since 1955 the scale has been used by psychology researchers as a standard numerical measurement of mood. For your convenience, ten separate cards are provided, each with a pair of emotionally descriptive words printed on it. Between the words is a scale from 1 to 5. To understand clearly how you will be using these pairings to assess your moods, take a look at the complete mood scale, printed below.

On the left are ten adjectives that describe low emotional states; on the right, each adjective refers to an emotional high. To see how the scale works, choose any one of the pairs that attracts your attention, whether or not it seems to reflect anything about your current mood. The number 3, halfway between the two words you have chosen, indicates an emotional midpoint between these two particular states. The number 1 denotes the lower end of the emotional scale—apathy, extreme nervousness, feelings of pessimism—and 5 signals the opposite—enthusiasm, calm, feelings of opti-

MOOD SCALE

RIGHT AT THIS MOMENT I FEEL:

Restless	I	2	3	4	5	Peaceful
Very uneasy	I	2	3	4	5	Very much at ease
Very nervous	I	2	3	4	5	Calm
Sad	I	2	3	4	5	Happy
Got the blues	I	2	3	4	5	Cheerful
Apprehensive	I	2	3	4	5	Confident
Apathetic	I	2	3	4	5	Enthusiastic
Heavy	I	2	3	4	5	Buoyant
Pessimistic	I	2	3	4	5	Optimistic
Lethargic	I	2	3	4	5	Peppy

mism. The numbers 2 and 4 help define your mood state with more precision.

Chances are that you are feeling a bit of initial resistance to this scale. Do the word choices accurately describe the feelings that are characteristic of your own daily emotional life? Well, probably not—and for good reason. We all develop our own uniquely personal languages. The word pairings on this scale have to be general, for use by everyone. After a little practice, you will see that these very general terms will take on particular meaning for your own emotional states.

In addition, they can give you specific insights into the exact nature of your feelings. Wade Silverman, Ph.D., sports psychologist and chairman of the Psychology Department at Barry College in Miami, Florida, warns that most people equate mood with emotion . . . and do so in a deceptively simplistic way. In other words, most of us can recognize when we're up or down, but that's of little help in putting us at the right point on Maharam's Curve.

What does "feeling good" mean to a particular person on a particular day in a particular situation? "Happy" because of a shot from Cupid's bow, or "productive" because of an unexpected promotion on the job? When you feel "down" do you really mean "angry" . . . "hostile" . . . "disappointed"? Your mood has as much to do with outside factors as with your body's activity, and is much more complex and ineffable than our facial expressions and casual language about feelings can ever suggest.

Finally, you may be daunted by the idea of dealing with this scale several times a day. Have faith. You'll learn to assess your mood in seconds. You'll also learn things about your changing feelings that will encourage you to keep testing the inner you.

The Scale: Step by Step

When new patients come for the first visit, as you've seen, we first discuss motivation. Next, even though they might not yet understand perfectly why they want to start an exercise program, I familiarize them with the mood cards. I explain this mood scale and ask them to start practicing at home as soon as possible. Immediately is preferable.

Here is the procedure, step by step:

1. *Shuffle the cards.* After plotting your mood scale several times, it's possible that you could let the familiar order of the pairings affect your answers. From the beginning, it's a good idea to get in the habit of changing them around.
2. *Go through the cards fairly quickly* and jot down a score, 1 through 5, for each pair. Don't ponder. First impressions are best. Also, you will feel more confident about your answers when you have done the scale several times. Don't worry if you feel a little vague about your answers when you first start out.
3. *Add the ten separate scores* and divide the total by 10, then subtract 3. This number reflects your mood at this

moment. Consider the range of possible scores. If you were feeling emotionally high on every word pairing, the total of your cards would be the maximum 50. Divided by 10 with 3 subtracted, this total would give you a score of 2. That's pretty happy. A score of -2 would be the opposite extreme.

4. *Write down your score, the date, and the time* in a diary or small notebook that you can carry around easily during the day. For the next week or so, do the mood scale when you wake up, sometime during the day, and just before you go to sleep—more frequently if you like. Pretty soon you will begin to see a very clear graph of your mood swings. Some people tend to wake up as -2, with a bearish growl, and leap up a point or two after morning coffee. You may be the type of person who almost always greets the day with optimism, beginning at the peak level $(+2)$. No pattern is right or wrong.

MOOD RANGE

	$+2$
Positive moods	$+1$
	0 (neutral mood)
	-1
Negative moods	-2

The point of assessing your moods is to find a way of melding them with your exercise program, as I will explain later.

5. *Think.* The mood scale is only a tool; you still have to do the hard work of really looking into yourself. Just as we used motivation as a tool for finding your feelings, you will use the mood scale as a tool by assigning a number to these feelings. With practice, you will learn to listen to your mind and your body. You will be ready

DIARY PAGE NO. I

DATE	TIME	TIME	TIME	TIME	TIME	TIME

Fill in times that are convenient to you at the top and record your mood scores daily.

to take the next step and actually place yourself on Maharam's Curve.

The five steps described above should give most people little trouble when there is a strong, sincere commitment to the difficult work of understanding your mood. Let me digress for a moment, however, to discuss the special case of the so-called "Type A" personality, a condition that has received an enormous amount of attention in the media and our everyday world.

The Type A Syndrome

If you are a Type A personality, you are going to have to try especially hard to analyze your emotions accurately. Characteristically, this type of person is unable to connect emotion immediately with its causative event. For example, a Type A might hear of the death of a good friend, suddenly feel sad several hours later, and not be able to understand why his or her mood has changed. Whatever the emotion, this inability to link cause with emotional effect is a danger sign. Other indications are commonly known: the hard-driving workaholic behavior, the stratospherically high levels of anxiety, the inability to relax and smell the roses.

Toward exercise, the Type A individual is as driven and as emotionally isolated as in every other activity. Our Type A sees the workout as necessary but not enjoyable, a kind of preventive medicine required by yet another unyielding demand of human living. Exercise is the means to an end, never an end in itself.

By definition, Maharam's Curve flies in the face of this attitude. I want everyone to enjoy exercise, to want to come back for more. If you are Type A, you are going to have to make a special effort to hear what I'm saying, beginning with a special effort to investigate your hidden, suppressed, too-long-ignored emotions.

The Type B Syndrome

In contrast with Type A, a Type B individual is typically low-keyed and relaxed, not as super charged or ambitious. In my experience, Type Bs approach Maharam's Curve as they do everything else, methodically and open-mindedly, curious to see what will happen. They don't seem to have any special difficulties associated with learning my program, nor any special affinities. In other words, having a Type B personality seems to be neither a help nor a hindrance.

How the Cards Work

If you still find yourself resistant to the idea of the word pairings, I can only take note of my own experience. Over and over, patients who let the barriers fall find that the cards work for them.

One of my patients, Sara L., a 20-year-old Broadway "gypsy" (dancer in the chorus line), introduced herself to me as the "bitchy type" and said that her analyst agreed with that assessment. (Soon, so would I.) Nonetheless, I saw that she sincerely wanted to learn to enjoy exercise, in part because keeping her body fit was essential to her career, and she faced long hours of strenuous effort as part of the package.

She was true to her self-described nature when I brought up the subject of the mood scale cards. "Forget about it," she sneered. I hung in there, giving one of my pep talks. "You just sit down with the cards and shuffle through them." "No way!" She bought everything except the cards. Determined to win her over, I suggested she take a six-foot-wide piece of white posterboard, write the numbers 1 through 5 across the top of it, then lay it down on the floor with the cards lined up along each side. She could dance back and forth over the posterboard, selecting the cards and placing them with the appropriate number at the top, according to her mood.

For two days, the dancer tried my bizarre suggestion. Then the phone rang. "This is nuts. It takes too much time." I sensed she was hooked. "Fine," I laughed, "I couldn't agree with you more. Why not just sit down with the cards and shuffle through them?"

She did. By the end of the second week of practice, she reported that her mood had elevated. Friends, she reported, said she was much easier to deal with. Though I never met her analyst or anyone else who knew her, she did stop bragging about what a bitch she was. Happy in her exercise program, she no longer needed that particular self-defeating crutch to explain her unhappiness and low self-esteem.

Jennifer B., a 47-year-old novelist, also objected strongly to the cards at first.

"Those cards just aren't me," she explained.

"That's not it."

"Well, I can't relate to those words. They're not precise enough."

"I'm not asking you to relate to them. Just make a pop judgment, get a number, and go on." Perhaps this advice sounds contradictory after I have previously emphasized how important it is to understand your feelings and your motivations clearly in the beginning. The mood scale requires a different approach, though. You are trying to get a quick fix on fleeting moods. If you tediously analyze each pairing of the cards, you can't capture the feeling of the moment. More likely you'll destroy it. The cards will average out, giving you the information you need for Maharam's Curve. They're not tools for in-depth analysis.

In the case of this novelist, of course, precise definition of feelings could be considered basic to her career, but I sensed that something else was in the way. Other writers have not resisted so doggedly.

"Could there be another reason why you're resisting?"

She didn't think so.

But at our second meeting she was able to explain that she had been able to nail down what bothered her. If this mood scale really worked, she feared, she might learn too much about her hidden emotions, a knowledge that could make her lose control.

"What if I'm depressed every time I talk to my mother on the phone? I don't want to know that. What if I'm relieved every time my husband has to work late? I don't want to know these things. I need control of my emotions." (Let me make clear that she tended to express herself rather dramatically. If she had really been experiencing depression or other emotional problems, I would have referred her to a professional analyst. These days, it's not unusual for laypeople to use clinical terms in a flip way, so one has to listen carefully.)

"Fine," I said. "If you want to control your emotional life, the mood scale will empower you. If you really know what you feel, you will learn how to deal with it."

Hesitantly, she agreed to try the cards that were so difficult to relate to. I don't know whether or not she gained more control of her emotional life; that wasn't my area of expertise or concern. Rather, I was able to watch as she learned to control her exercise patterns and grasp the secret of attaining her exercise high.

Checking Your Moods

These two anecdotes probably don't apply directly to you, but I hope they affirm my point. Whatever your unease about using the mood scale, I'm willing to bet that you can use it well if you suppress your doubts. I have not yet had a patient who could not learn to benefit from the word pairings on the cards.

To become proficient in using the mood scale, you have to start checking your moods three times a day, without fail. Make things easy for yourself by using the same kind of memory tricks you use when you have to take medication several times a day. For example, you can key your three mood assessments to meals, checking before (or after) breakfast, lunch, and dinner. Or you can link the scale to your work schedule: a teacher might always take the second test of the day after fourth-period class; a computer programmer in a large corporation might schedule a test with each mandated coffee break, and so forth.

The important thing is to get in the habit, and let the mood assessing become second nature. You will find, I'm pretty sure, that the process will become a fascinating game. You are learning to recognize the individual pattern of your own ups and downs.

DIARY PAGE NO. 2

DATE	TIME	TIME	TIME

Check your moods at three consistent times per day.

And start using the lingo of Maharam's Curve. "I'm minus-one today, Doc," a patient will say to me, when he's feeling blue. That kind of comment gets us somewhere. Depression I leave to experts, but I can do something about a mood level that's − 1. And you can too. Soon you will be speaking quite naturally in this language: "I woke up minus-two, but I was plus-one-and-a-half after I ran for an hour." "I'm only plus-one this afternoon, after my workout, so maybe I need to vary my pace in order to reach a higher mood."

When your friends and family members start asking, "What are you talking about?" you will realize that you've slipped into this new way of thinking . . . and you're well on your way to life on Maharam's Curve.

And when *they* start using these terms, you will begin to understand each other on an entirely new level—as well as reinforce your shared commitment to the continuing work and pleasure of exercise.

Joining the Curve

Once you learn to track your moods, it's time to apply this knowledge to your exercise program. As I have noted, building upon the insight of *New York Times* writer William Stockton, the "power" in my program is precisely this connection between mood and actual exercise regimen. Now that you've learned how to recognize the former, you can apply that knowledge to the latter: in other words, you will assess your moods in order to devise an exercise program that will put you on your individual Curve. In order to implement the linkage, it's important for you to remember two essential points.

First, the early phase of any new exercise routine is likely to be difficult physically and emotionally. The gains aren't immediately apparent; the effort is. You cannot expect to go racing up the hump in Maharam's Curve to pure exercise bliss in the first session, the first week, or even the first few weeks. Be patient.

Second, you don't need to make things more difficult by starting when you're already in a low mood. That's a prescription for failure. Nor should you begin your new exercise program when you're feeling on top of the world. If you just won the Super Bowl, for example, you don't want to consider the moment of victory as your baseline mood level zero. That way, you have no place to go but down. That's not a curve; that's a chute. Your goal should be to start your program when you're psychologically at neutral, level zero on the mood scale. Don't worry if you're *slightly* negative or *slightly* positive. Consider yourself at mood level zero if you're in that ballpark.

From that point, you will notice your mood swerving upward or downward as you exercise. If your mood drops toward the negative end of the scale, there is some problem with your program. I'll talk about that in a later chapter. If, as is usually the case, your mood begins to rise as you become confident in your exercise program, you will be able to chart the positive consequences of your activity. You will want to repeat the activity that makes you feel so good. You will begin to learn which aspects of your workout routine are the most beneficial to your mood.

Remember this warning: you have to keep doing the cards regularly or you will be acting upon inadequate or incorrect information. You won't be able simply to "feel" your moods, not for the specific demands of the Curve; you have to keep doing the minimal work of the cards and learn to feel comfortable with the task.

Now, while you become used to that concept, let's pause a moment for some important background information. Because it concerns basic nutrition, you may think it's boring, and you may think it's old news; I believe the next short chapter will show that you would be wrong on both counts.

CHAPTER FIVE

PREPARING YOURSELF FOR THE CURVE I: EATING SMART

You don't run 26 miles at five minutes a mile on good looks and a secret recipe.

—Frank Shorter

Put aside the image of the Curve for a moment, and think instead of a circle, the shape that suggests perfect balance and equilibrium. You will not reach your optimum exercise rhythm until all of the physical and mental factors are as precisely and beautifully balanced as the ideal circle.

In this chapter and others to follow, I will talk about some of these factors. Because of the vastly improved and broadened research of recent years, much is now known about maximizing your exercise potential, about avoiding injury, or about eating the proper foods in the proper way. Still, expert knowledge can only point the way toward the balance that is right for you, the circle that is your own personal state of perfect equilibrium. You will have to find it for yourself by testing the advice I give you, altering the general guidelines to suit your own situation. You will not really get on the Curve until you achieve a balance of the many elements of proper exercise, beginning with the correct preparation.

How the Right Food Helps

Your success on the Curve will be enhanced by proper nutrition. Conversely, you cannot expect to reach your maximum potential if you handicap your body by giving it insufficient or inappropriate fuel. Whether you are returning to regular exercise or beginning a program for the first time, how and what you eat and drink will directly affect your performance. Of course, these principles apply to everyone, including sedentary people, but you will be especially sensitive to the consequences of improper nutrition when you are riding the Curve. You will be so aware of your physical condition and your feelings that you will begin to recognize, probably with horror, what bad diet does to your body— and your future.

Your level of physical performance at this moment is a combination of the influence of three factors. First, there's Mother Nature's legacy from the gene pool. Accept it. On that score, the lottery's over.

But the other two factors—physical training and nutrition—can be controlled. We've been talking about physical training throughout this book, but exercise is inextricably linked with nutrition. When you understand your body's nutritional needs, and serve them well, you begin to achieve greater physical heights. Nutrition is the lifeblood of exercise.

A well-balanced diet gives you the strength necessary for working out. It also helps enhance your performance and, from the perspective of Maharam's Curve, speeds your achievement of the exercise high. A balanced diet is a literal balance of the appropriate amounts of essential nutrients (proteins, carbohydrates, fats) and the required vitamins and minerals. In sports nutrition, we do not count calories in designing an individual's diet, because caloric intake is a meaningless standard. For example, two people of approximately the same age, height, build, and weight may require a totally different amount of calories to maintain weight and exercise vitality.

Perhaps your eyes are beginning to glaze over now because you think you've heard it all before, beginning at your mother's knee. The message comes at us constantly, from school nurses, from Slim Goodbody on "Captain Kangaroo," from our personal physicians, and from newspaper articles about the latest scientific study. In my case, there was the additional input from my years in medical school and working with professional and amateur athletes.

Even so, I was in for a surprise when I recently took a coffee break with Merle Best, a registered dietician who was formerly the nutritionist for the New York Giants. Merle knows how to manipulate diet in order to enhance athletic performance. As she pointed out to me as we ate our bagels, the nutrients in what we eat are fuel for the increased physical activity of an exercise program. But we cannot, she warned, suddenly start filling up the tank to the brim and hope to go long distances right away. Instead, moderation in changing diet is the key, just as it is in developing a new exercise routine. We have to work slowly toward a goal. Sudden changes in diet can have detrimental effects on your exercise program and delay your progress toward achieving the Curve. My brief discussion here is only an overview; Appendix A, page 199, gives a complete rundown of The Balanced Diet.

Note to experienced exercisers: don't be overconfident about your ability to manage your own diet. In a recent study of 93 elite female athletes, researchers discovered that many of the women who considered themselves energy efficient were in fact risking nutrition deficiency by eating too few calories (and thus too few nutrients) for good health. They were also more prone to eating disorders than less active women and therefore predisposed to amenorrhea, stress fractures, and other injuries. In short, the skilled, knowledgeable, and successful athletes in this study group did not always eat properly, even though most were convinced that they knew the basics of eating for fitness.

Often, experienced athletes will assume that their performance is diminishing because they are overtraining when the problem is actually undereating. Inability to keep up regular pace in a race or an exercise routine, higher pulse rate the following day, fatigue, irritability, depression, insomnia, intolerance of pain—these classic symptoms of overtraining can also be a warning that you are not eating enough carbohydrates.

By the way, everything I'm about to say on the subject of exercise diets applies as well to good eating for everyone and to eating for a healthy heart.

Water/Fluids

Water, one of the purest nutrients, is perhaps the most critical for humans, because it is essential to metabolizing energy, controlling body temperature, and eliminating metabolic wastes. Although few laypersons or professionals actually follow the rule, you should drink the equivalent of eight glasses of water every day to maintain body water, whether you exercise or not. After all, fully 60 percent of the healthy body is water.

Perhaps surprisingly, though, the loss of only 2 percent of that huge amount will bring about a measurable decrease in your exercise performance. Your muscles, dependent upon that essential fuel, will stop functioning properly. Generally speaking, you will lose that 2 percent through sweat in an average, strenuous, 45-minute workout. So, because it is vital to keep your blood and muscles hydrated, you should replace fluid at least every 15 minutes as you exercise.

In some popular publications, you will see the following formula suggested for runners as a good guideline for all strenuous exercise: To find the number of ounces lost, multiply your body weight, in pounds, by your running speed in miles per hour, then divide the total by 28.5. For example, at a nine-minute mile (or 6 8/9 mph) a 150-pound runner will use up 35 ounces per hour: 150 times 6 8/9 divided by 28.9 equals 35.

This is far too complicated! I prefer a simpler method, which requires only that you weigh yourself before and after exercise. For each pound you lose during a session, drink one pint of liquid replacement, watered down to suit your own taste. In hot weather, you should drink water more often, both before and during your exercise routine. The cooler the water, the more quickly it will empty from the stomach and be absorbed by your dehydrating body.

You can't rely upon common sense in deciding how quickly to replenish body fluids. Thirst is simply not an accurate indicator of the level of dehydration. In fact, reliance upon thirst will probably cause you to replace no more than one-half to two-thirds of the fluid necessary. When you become seriously dehydrated, you may experience such symptoms as dry mouth, chills, muscle cramps, and a severe sense of fatigue. Long before then, you should have been replenishing your body water. Depending upon the form of exercise you prefer, you can devise tricks for keeping yourself adequately hydrated during a workout. You should practice them before competition. During a race, for example, you might choose to slow down to a fast walk at the water stop and quaff eight ounces of fluid. You can cut down on spillage by using a drinking straw especially designed to be worn on a chain around your neck. Or you can pick up the paper or plastic cup, bend it into a V shape, and take small sips as you keep moving for a couple hundred yards.

As experienced exercisers know, appropriate fluid replacement includes restoring the natural balance of your body's electrolytes. This term, which has been used and abused in many popular articles during the past decade or so, is simply a collective designation for essential elements: sodium, potassium, chloride. Undoubtedly, Madison Avenue has made you aware again and again of the various brand-name replacement drinks that have been specifically created for athletes and exercisers. If such products have sodium and glucose, the fluid will be more rapidly absorbed in the intestines, giving you faster fluid replacement and faster recovery from exercise stress. What are the advantages of commercially made rapid-replacement beverages? The sodium helps you retain the thirst drive better than plain water, the flavoring is more attractive to the taste buds, and the glucose makes the body's absorption of water an active process rather than just passive diffusion, causing extra pumps in the cell membrane to kick in.

On the other hand, do not overdo it. Studies of cyclists have shown that the commercial drinks empty as quickly as water from your stomach only so long as the concentration of carbohydrates is no more than about 8 percent. With this level of concentration, the carbos go to work quickly, boosting performance and staving off exhaustion. Drinking too much of the replacement fluid, however, can cause stomach discomfort. The earlier you begin to drink the fluid after a lengthy, strenuous exercise period, the less likely it is that you will experience stomach upset. Drink early and often for best results.

Many professional teams prefer Gatorade, but I have found that it is no less effective when mixed with water, one-third Gatorade to two-thirds water, or according to taste. The product is now available in three different versions: Gatorade, Gatorlode, and Gatorpro. The manufacturer suggests that Gatorade, which is simply a fluid replacement, be used with the following guidelines: 4 to 8 ounces immediately before exercise, 4 to 10 ounces every 15 to 20 minutes during exercise, and 8 to 16 ounces after exercise.

Another fluid replacement and energy drink, EXCEED, is comparable to Gatorade except that it has a glucose polymer; Gatorade has glucose and fructose. The product known as Gatorlode is designed to be a carbo-loader. The manufacturer recommends the following guidelines for using Gatorlode: 8 to 16 ounces 2 hours before your exercise session, 12 to 24 ounces within half an hour after exercise, 12 ounces with meals, and 12 to 24 ounces between meals. Similarly, EXCEED has created a product, EXCEED High Carbohydrate Source, that provides a concentrated supply of calories derived from carbohydrates. Gatorpro is described by the manufacturer as a meal supplement. These guidelines are recommended: 8 to 16 ounces 2 hours before exercise, 8 ounces after exercise, 8 ounces with meals, and 8 ounces between meals. EXCEED has a similar product.

Some professionals like to use still other replacement fluids, including glucose polymer drinks (e.g., EXCEED and Max) with a chemical variation of glucose that does not dissipate throughout the body as quickly as plain glucose. Remember that after your exercise period, or a tough game of tennis or racquetball, your main objective is to replace water and electrolytes.

Carbohydrates

For energy during exercise, muscles prefer carbohydrates, or "carbos" in athletes' slang, but don't get carried away. Recently, a lot of attention has been focused on carbos and their effect upon performance, including the famed pre-marathon carbo-loading (see page 69). Even so, almost all the athletes I work with were not originally getting enough carbos for their exercise. When I increase the amount of carbos they intake, they not only perform better and longer but also feel better doing it. Why? Because the body breaks the carbos down to glucose which, in turn, is used by the body's cells to provide energy. With these energy stores available, your workout can continue at a steady pace. Because the nerve cells are also included, the nervous system is energized and keeps your spirits up, your outlook fresh.

Good food sources for carbohydrates include root vegetables (like potatoes), grains (oat, wheat, corn, rice), grain products (breads, pasta), and dried beans and peas. These carbo sources are known as complex carbohydrates, because of the additional nutritional benefits provided, including protein, vitamins, iron, and fiber. That's why pastas and other grain products are so popular with athletes for pre-workout meals.

Contrary to popular belief, high-carbohydrate foods are not necessarily fattening, so long as we keep the definitions straight. For example, some people have a very loose idea of the meaning of the word "pasta." One of my patients complained to me that he had horrible reactions when he followed my advice to eat pasta the night before running. Immediately after his run, he would experience severe stomach cramps, virtually doubling over from the pain.

"Doc, I can't understand it," he said. "I eat nothing but pasta the night before."

Yes, but what kind of pasta was he eating? Spaghetti and meatballs. Obviously, the pasta itself was not the culprit. The toppings in many popular pasta dishes (butter, heavy meat, or cheese sauces) are the source of the extra, and unnecessary, calories that can cause weight gain, not to mention my patient's terrible experience.

Sugar, or sucrose, is another source of carbohydrates, as are lactose in milk and fructose in fruits and fruit juices. Sucrose, however, holds few other nutrients.

Carbo-Loading: Yes or No?

Now, a cautionary word on carbo-loading, which has become a popular ritual for many long-distance and endurance athletes. Carbo-loading is *only* beneficial for endurance exercise. For short-term athletics, no matter how intensely you exercise, it has absolutely no value. To be precise, any sports or activity consisting of less than two hours of continuous, noninterrupted exertion does not benefit from carbo-loading (also known as glycogen-loading, because glycogen is the form in which the body stores glucose and is your principal muscle fuel). In a study at Ohio State University, researchers found that an 80 percent carbohydrate diet did not help swimmers improve their speed in 50-meter and 200-meter endurance tests. Swimmers on a 43 percent carbohydrate diet performed just as well as the carbo-loaders.

Carbo-loading is a way of manipulating the diet and amount of exercise in order to increase and maintain a steady store of glycogen in the muscles. For example, many endurance athletes load up on pasta and potatoes just before a big race to give their muscles an extra boost. Some studies have shown that there are benefits from carbo-loading in long-distance running and cross-country skiing, but there is a possible down side. When a muscle stores glycogen, it also stores water at a ratio of approximately one-to-two. This additional water can cause stiffness and some loss of flexibility.

Before we go on to discuss carbo-loading, you should also be aware of this important warning: replacing glycogen after a strenuous workout will not necessarily return you to your normal performance level. Muscle fuel, in other words, is not the whole story of recovery; rest is also essential. Because factors other than loss of glycogen can cause muscle fatigue, you must be sure to let your muscles recover adequately after each workout.

Early forms of carbo-loading caused adverse effects, such as chest pains, muscle damage, stomach pain, weight gain, increased water retention, and depression. Today, experts advise that you ease your workouts during the final three days before any endurance event two hours or more in length and make carbos about 70 percent of your caloric total (about 10 grams of carbohydrates for each kilogram of body weight each day). Your store of glycogen will increase by 1.5 to 2.6 times its normal.

If you are an endurance athlete and decide to try carbo-loading for yourself, experiment during your routine training. For runners who don't like the feeling of gorging themselves with extra pasta, I've found that Gatorlode is a wonderful alternative for carbo-loading before an endurance competition. Three 12-ounce glasses of the drink provide 810 calories—roughly the equivalent of 4 baked potatoes, 2 plates of pasta, and 4 slices of bread. There is no fat or protein in Gatorlode; all of the calories are carbohydrates. By contrast, a cup of pasta is 81 percent carbohydrates, 13 percent protein, and 6 percent fat. EXCEED's manufacturer believes that its High Carbohydrate Source, a powder to be mixed with water, provides 230 grams of carbos per quart, roughly the equivalent of 13 slices of white bread, 10 medium-sized baked potatoes, or 7 cups of enriched spaghetti. In the three days before a strenuous contest, carbo-loaders can eschew the food bulk and instead drink two or three 12-ounce glasses of Gatorlode each day. My patients who don't like pasta-loading tell me that they feel "pumped" with this drink. After a race, they are able to replace lost glycogen by drinking 12 to 24 ounces of Gatorlode within half an hour or so. Whatever kind of carbo-loading you choose, however, don't try it for the first time on the day before a big race!

In fact, it's a good general rule to follow the advice of Gordon Bloch, who was in 1988 the New York Road Runners Club Runner of the Year: "Trust your appetite. Don't change your diet before a race, but be sure to eat plenty of carbohydrates. Avoid eating a fatty meal the night before, since fat digests more slowly than carbohydrate and may make you feel sluggish on race morning. If you drink coffee on race morning—which is okay—make sure your drink water, too, to avoid dehydration."

My standard breakfast recommendation for the morning of a race, when pressed by my patients, includes cereal (avoid high fiber) with skim or lactose-free milk, toast with honey or jam, and a glass of orange juice or water.

Protein

Protein, a very versatile nutrient, is necessary on a daily basis. Not only is it important to the growth and repair of muscle tissue, it also affects just about every other structural tissue and all of the organs in your body. It also produces antibodies to fight infections and hormones to regulate body and neuromuscular function.

If you are an active adult, you probably do not need additional protein to enhance performance. Your total protein needs are met by your normal daily diet. In fact, protein consumed above and beyond the body's requirements for energy and muscle repair will be converted to fat and stored as excess calories.

According to the recommended dietary allowance (RDA) for a 200-pound male, daily protein intake should be 73 grams. If you are "bulking up" to increase your muscle mass, an additional 20 grams or so may be necessary. Remember, to maintain weight, protein intake should be 1.2 grams/kilograms daily; to increase muscle mass, 1.5 grams/kilograms daily.

Foods rich in protein and essential amino acids come from animal sources, including meat, fish, poultry, milk, cheese, and eggs. Some vegetable sources (dried beans, nuts, grains, pasta) also provide proteins, but without the amino acids. A combination of animal and vegetable proteins is best for the athlete's table.

Vitamins

It is well established that people who exercise regularly get all the nutrients their bodies need by eating smart and maintaining body weight. But we live in a world of people too busy to get the proper calories every day. For these individuals, Merle Best recommends any multivitamin mineral that can provide about 100 percent of the U.S. recommended daily allowance.

Some athletes have special needs, however, which must be considered for maximum vitamin requirements. For example, people in weight-controlled sports or endurance athletes require greater amounts of specific vitamins or minerals. These can be supplemented by multivitamins that include iron, vitamin C, or thiamin, depending upon the energy expenditure and the nature of the sport.

On the other hand, megavitamins are totally unnecessary. They don't provide more energy or promote a better performance. In fact, taking mega doses of any vitamin supplement can be dangerous.

If you eat a healthy diet, exercise regularly, and feel good, you don't need to supplement your vitamin intake. If you have *any* questions about vitamin or mineral needs or feel you may need supplementation, consult a registered dietician—if possible, one specializing in sports nutrition—or a sports medicine specialist.

Calories

Calories are units of energy the body uses to function and perform. Adequate caloric intake will allow the athlete to maintain his or her body weight. Too few calories will result in a loss of energy, which affects performance. Too many calories will make the body convert calories to fat for storage, causing the dreaded weight gain.

Exercise is the best way to maintain your body weight or even lose weight, because it burns the calories that fuel your body. If you burn as many calories as you ingest, your weight remains stable; if you burn more than you eat, you will lose weight. Put another way, exercise can boost your metabolism, the rate at which your body ordinarily uses up calories.

There's an extra bonus for the exerciser: even at rest, you will burn more calories than a sedentary person. How can this be? Everyone's metabolic rate rises after a meal, using up calories, but researchers have discovered that the rise is higher for people who exercise regularly, even at a moderate level of training. The fit person loses extra calories even when resting. As a general guideline, a total expenditure each week of 2,000 calories will keep the average person fit and healthy.

Maharam's Curve is not a program of weight loss, but at least ten times a day I get asked, "How many calories will I burn biking, or jogging, or swimming . . . ?" The answers are shown in Appendix B, page 201.

Diet Problems

If, during your exercise, you feel tired day after day or have nausea, vomiting, or other gastrointestinal symptoms, or if you have trouble with your weight, you may need to discuss your dietary patterns with a sports medicine physician or nutritionist. I think it is very important, when choosing a sports nutritionist, to find someone who is a registered dietician or has had similarly appropriate training in nutrition. As Sue Luke, spokeswoman for the American Dietetic Association, says wryly, "We're no longer stuck in the basement with the white stockings and the hair net. Today, people are recognizing that we *are* the nutrition experts. There are renal dietitians, diabetic dietitians, and now sports and cardiovascular. It's a field whose time has come."

A registered dietician has passed an exam certifying a high level of knowledge and education in nutrition. In addition, the American Dietetic Association requires a total of 75 hours of continuing education every five years after the initial certification. Be aware that a lot of people out there are selling something and really don't know a thing about nutrition. Within the ADA there is a specialized group called SCAN (Sports and Cardiovascular Nutritionists), registered dieticians who are knowledgeable about sports nutrition and can help you. Contact the American Dietetic Association (see Appendix C for the address) to ask for the names of members of SCAN in your area.

As we move into a description of your preparations for exercise, remember that it is only with proper diet that your body and your mind can function together in harmony. You have to work on your diet in order to fuel your personal firepower and get the necessary impetus for getting on the Curve.

Eye on the Circle

All this nutritional information falls within the circle I mentioned at the beginning of this chapter. If you are obsessive about carbo-loading at the expense of other aspects of nutrition, if you neglect mood assessment because you're focusing exclusively on revving up your exercise pace, your program will be thrown out of balance. As you read on, remember that the key to long-range growth and development is proper balance. Everything in this chapter should be seen as part of the ideal circle. Maharam's Curve is, first and last, about finding and maintaining the equilibrium that sustains mental and physical well-being.

PREPARING YOURSELF FOR THE CURVE II: REVVING THE BODY

Once again, let us think of the circle, our image of balance and equilibrium. In this chapter, we're going to look at several specific factors in achieving and maintaining that balance by preventing injury and undue stress. Stretching, for example, an essential preparation for physical well-being, is often misunderstood; I'll explain how it properly fits into our circle. Warming up is important, as is "warming down," a concept that is not as familiar as it should be to athletes and exercisers, whether unpracticed or experienced. Medical advice and proper equipment are also important in ensuring that an exercise program does not threaten your well-being by leaving you vulnerable to preventable injury.

Experienced athletes know the importance of preventing injuries during a workout by stretching beforehand. We've all seen weekend joggers duly stretching before running off down the road or through a city park. Unfortunately, as I am reminded frequently when a patient comes into my office in great pain, it is true in pre-exercise stretching (as in much else) that a little knowledge is a dangerous thing. You have to understand the purpose of stretching in order to make it work well for you. And you have to be current with the latest research: recent discoveries have led to a reevaluation of the advice that was regularly doled out for runners, say, just a few years ago.

The basic misunderstanding is that too many people assume that stretching is virtually the same thing as warming up for exercise. They know that the body, like a car with a cold transmission on an icy morning, needs to warm up, because muscles are cold and tight. So far, true enough. You can even picture your muscles as salt-water taffy: yank a piece when it's cold, and it breaks, but when it's warm, it pulls out nice and evenly. But that is exactly the point. Stretching is like pulling the taffy, so you have to warm up *before* you stretch. I can't emphasize this distinction strongly enough. Stretching and warming up are equally important before you exercise, but they are separate activities.

Just as important, you have to stretch and warm *down* after your workout, taking time to return your muscles to their pre-exercise state. (Some exercisers call this "cooling down," but, as you'll see below, "warming down" is really a much more accurate term.)

All of these essential injury-preventing factors are incorporated in a very simple five-point program developed by New York Giants team physician Dr. Allan Levy, who virtually invented the "warm up/warm down" concept.

LEVY'S FIVE-POINT "WARM UP/WARM DOWN"

Let's imagine going through each one:

1. Warm up: Before stretching, you want to do exactly what the term "warm up" suggests—raise your body temperature by 1½ to 2 degrees. The activity doesn't matter—a slow jog, some calisthenics, stationary biking—and the goal is clear: once you begin to sweat, you've warmed up.

This critically important step will make muscle fiber, tendons, and ligaments more pliable and elastic. Joints begin to secrete more fluid, easing wear and tear, and your reaction time goes up, because the speed of the message from nerve to muscle is increased.

2. Stretching: To prevent injuries, only "static stretching" should be used. In this method, you stretch a part of the body to the maximum, without forcing, and hold for 10 to 20 seconds. Relax, then repeat the stretch three to five times. The increase in flexibility will decrease your internal resistance to your exercise, thus cutting down on fatigue and maximizing efficiency.

It's always best if you can stretch all parts of the body before working out. As Joe Morris puts it, "God did not create your arms one day and your legs the next." But you should pay special attention to those muscles used most in the exercise you choose. For example, tennis players should stretch both upper and lower areas, because of the nature of the demands of the game. For runners, walkers, and cyclists, the focus should be on the lower extremities: the lower back, gluteals, quadriceps, hamstrings, calves, and Achilles tendon. Baseball players, by contrast, need to pay most attention to stretching the upper extremities.

One warning: So-called "ballistic stretching," or bouncing, used to be popular among dancers and gymnasts but has been proved to be harmful. In theory, this type of stretching would provide even greater flexibility because the tendon is forced beyond its normal limit. Therein, it turns out, lay the danger. The forced stretching could tear muscle and tendon fibers, and in fact shorten the muscle. (For a good basic program of stretching exercises, turn to Appendix D for Bob Anderson's expert suggestions.)

3. Do your workout: I'll have a lot more to say about that in the next section.

4. Warm down: Your goal now that exercise is completed is to return your muscles to the preworkout state. Your temperature is above normal, of course, and you must use that diminishing heat and a diminishing rate of exercise to return your body to normal, *before* it cools off. That's why Dr. Levy's term, "warm down," is so accurately descriptive.

The warming down is a kind of bridge from intense activity to a state of rest; the easiest method, therefore, is simply to decrease your rate of activity, whatever it is. Or you can spend a few minutes jogging slowly down to a walk. Your heart rate level should be allowed to fall to normal. These few minutes are vital.

Consider what happens if you're a runner. Blood is pumped into the muscles of your legs, exactly where you need it, by your straining, fast-beating heart. That's great, as long as you keep running. When you stop suddenly, all that extra blood puddles in your legs. Your body doesn't have a very efficient mechanism for returning it quickly to the heart and brain. That's why a sudden stop makes you vulnerable to fainting or even a heart attack, especially if you're older. Warming down slowly will prevent that kind of episode.

Don't take this warning lightly. Even an experienced physician can take a terrible risk. A radiologist in his late fifties came to me some years ago when he wanted to start regular exercise. One of the most compulsive people I've ever met, he didn't want to take the time for an exercise test, and he wasn't interested in the Curve. He just wanted to get the outline for a strenuous program of running. As it turned out, he listened only to what he wanted to hear, completely ignoring my advice about warming down. After a hard run, with the veins in his legs dilated or expanded from the heat of exertion (vasodilation), he strode right into a hot shower . . . and suffered a heart attack. Because the heat of the water kept his leg veins dilated, the blood there could not return quickly enough to the heart and other organs. Fortunately, he survived the episode. He still runs. Now he warms down!

Another potential problem prevented by warming down is muscle soreness the next day or even a feeling of illness. When you are exercising, lactic acid builds up in your muscles, causing fatigue and burn. Keeping the blood circulating by warming down, you help the body wash the lactic acid out of your muscles.

Prevention of muscle pain, a sick feeling, fainting, or even a heart attack—this is strong enough encouragement, I'd think, for taking the few moments necessary to warm down.

5. Restretching: This period of stretching is probably even more important than pre-exercise stretching, because it will prevent soreness the next day. Your muscles have shortened from overuse during your workout; they need to be drawn out again, taffy-wise, to normal lengths. If you don't restretch, they will remain at the shorter length. Because your muscles are still warm, you will only have to spend a couple of minutes on restretching. As before, stretch to the maximum and hold it, but do not push past the point of pain.

Again, here are the five points explained above:

1. Warm up
2. Stretch
3. Workout
4. Warm down
5. Restretch

Your Target Heart Range

Before we go back to mood scales and the expected shape of Maharam's Curve, beginners and veteran exercisers alike need to learn about "target heart range." This is the heartbeat level you have to achieve during exercise in order to begin working your way from mood level zero on to the Curve.

If you have exercised before, you are probably familiar with this concept, because any aerobic training demands that you achieve your target heart range. "Becoming aerobic," and phrases of that sort, refers to maintaining this level of exercise for a required period of time.

Like practically all other exercise programs, Maharam's Curve requires that you push your heart rate to that range for at least 20 minutes three times a week. Otherwise, the exercise will not effectively work to strengthen your heart, and you will have no hope of moving out of the first phase of the three-phase Curve into Phases II and III.

Finding your own target heart range takes a bit of simple math. First, subtract your age from 220. Take the result and multiply it by 65 percent to find the lower end of your target range, by 85 percent to find the upper end. This is basic to making your exercise program work for you, so take a moment to do this step correctly.

Let these two examples be your guide:

If you are 30 years old, subtract 30 from 220 to get 190. When you multiply 190 by 65 percent (.65), the result is about 124 beats per minute—the lower end of your target heart range. When you multiply the same number, 190, by 85 percent (.85), the result is about 162 beats per minute.

Your personal range, therefore, is from 124 to 162 beats per minute. If your heart rate lies within that range for the entire 20 minutes of your exercise session, you are exercising effectively.

If you are 50 years old, subtract 50 from 220 to get 170.

When you multiply 170 by 65 percent (.65), the result is about 111 beats per minute—the lower end of your target heart range. When you multiply the same number, 170, by 85 percent (.85), the result is about 145 beats per minute. Your personal range, at age 50, is from 111 to 145 beats per minute.

Write it down, memorize it, tape it on your mirror—somehow, you must tattoo your target heart range into your memory in order to become the best-qualified judge of your own fitness program.

But how do you keep track of your heartbeat? You'll need a watch with a second hand so that you can count your pulse for ten seconds, then multiply the result by six to get your approximate number of heart beats per minute.

This sounds like the simplest of prescriptions, but it is not. For one thing, a simple math mistake can throw you way off. Be sure you count your pulse carefully for the entire ten seconds; be sure you multiply by six. Remember, concentration is extremely important for accuracy. Missing one beat in your ten-second sampling, for example, will throw off your total by six beats.

Taking an accurate pulse is not quite as easy for everybody as it looks in the medical dramas on TV. Some people tend to press down too hard, or they try the wrong place. With one arm held out, palm up, gently place the middle three fingers of your other hand on the thumb side of the forearm near your wrist. Move it around until you feel a strong pulse. In this as in all things, you will improve with practice; your fingers will become more sensitive to your pulse.

Do not make the fairly common error of using your

thumb to feel your pulse rate. The thumb itself has a pulse that can confuse you.

And don't dally. About 20 seconds after you stop strenuous activity, your heart rate will plummet. When you are monitoring your rate to see whether or not you've reached aerobic levels, it's crucial that you act quickly. You should take your pulse during the middle of your exercise period, for certain, and at other intervals, as convenient. It will be easier for runners, for example, to take readings frequently as they work out, but swimmers, say, will not have that option.

When a rate seems peculiar, there may not necessarily be cause for alarm. Aside from the possible errors I've noted, your rate can be affected in the short term by numerous different factors: warm weather, dehydration, eating and drinking, stimulants. Consider these possibilities when you count a rate that seems out of line. If you have any questions about an unusual rate, don't hesitate to call your physician for an evaluation. Never just write it off.

Getting Good Medical Advice

If you have never exercised before, it is also a good idea to see a sports medicine physician before you begin your program. A couple of anecdotes will help you see why:

One woman in her late thirties, a highly organized banker, felt that her concentration at work was suffering because she had stopped exercising regularly. Painful shin splints, once thought (erroneously) to be caused by jogging on the sidewalks of New York, had ended her workouts. Physicians who had not been trained in the biomechanics we study in sports medicine had not been able to help her; they assumed the damage was permanent or would inevitably recur with exercise.

She was highly motivated to find a better answer, however, and eventually, having read about sports medicine, sought me out. The problem was easily correctable. Because her ankle was pronating, her tibia twisted with each step. Orthotic devices in each shoe lifted her arches enough to eliminate the problem. She was soon jogging again, without pain, and working with renewed concentration on her climb up the corporate ladder.

Another executive, a fit-looking 34-year-old man who had perhaps not always paced himself on his long, strenuous runs as well as he should, came to me with so-called "runner's knee." In this condition, the back of the knee cap has been worn down. Like the banker, he felt that lack of regular exercise was affecting his efficiency and his mood; he was depressed by the fear of never being able to work out again. I have to admit that it is a privilege to have such a patient, for the remedy for his problem was also simple: an appropriate orthotic combined with a quadrocept exercise program easily corrected his biomechanical problem. In addition, the right set of exercises made it possible for him to get into the first phase of Maharam's Curve and gradually return to the kind of exercising he missed so much.

Then there was Fred, a very earnest young man working in his father's firm who was something of an overachiever. He called during the first phase of the Curve in great alarm. He was following my advice to the letter, but something inexplicable was happening: the more strenuously he exercised, the blacker his toenails became. Had I ever heard of this horrifying exercise-induced disease?

Well, no, but fortunately, Fred's problem was not serious. Painstakingly careful to select the correct equipment, as I had suggested, he had bought a pair of brand-new Nikes that fit perfectly. Unfortunately, he hadn't remembered my warning that, for strenuous workouts, running shoes should be one half-size larger than for normal usage. Once he had the appropriately larger Nikes on his feet, Fred's unusual condition disappeared.

In fact, let us digress on a subject that is no digression at all: choosing the right athletic shoes is a major factor in preventing discomfort, pain, and possible injuries during strenuous exercise. Podiatrist John McNerney, who regularly writes about physical fitness for the *New York Times*, has come up with five guidelines for getting the right fit when you choose exercise shoes:

MCNERNEY'S FIVE RULES FOR BUYING ATHLETIC SHOES

1. Tip of shoe should be ¼-inch to ½-inch past end of the longest toe, generally the width of one thumbnail. Using your thumbnail works because a person with small fingers is likely to have small feet, a larger person will have correspondingly larger fingers and feet. In addition, the larger foot will swell proportionately after exercise. (Usually, the thumbnail gauge will yield a half-size larger than normal size, but in some cases it will be a whole size larger.)
2. Widest part of foot should lie comfortably in the widest part of the shoe.
3. Stand and lean down to run thumb over the widest part of the foot. The shoe at that point should have play, not feel tightly stretched.
4. When the shoe is snugly tied, there should be no play in the heel.
5. Always fit your shoes at the end of the day, when the foot is largest, because it has swelled.

In the three cases I've described, and many like them, it would have been disastrous for the exercisers to continue working out, despite the pain, until grave, irreversible damage was done. (It's surprising how many people are driven enough to do just that. Type As on the march!) It would have been unfortunate, too, if they had simply given up, since a professional evaluation could help them return to regular exercise.

Recently, the American Running and Fitness Association produced even more sophisticated guidelines for buying running shoes, specifically. For a printout of the running shoe that will match the precise needs of your foot, you can call them at 1-800-776-ARFA. If you send a long, self-addressed, stamped envelope, they will mail you a free brochure about choosing a running shoe for yourself (see their address in Appendix C).

As we go to the Curve itself, I hope that you will follow my advice about getting an evaluation before you start your exercise program. Unlike the banker, executive, and Fred, you might not be aware of physical problems that could lead to permanent damage.

CHAPTER SEVEN

VISUALIZING THE CURVE: AN OVERVIEW

At last, properly prepared for a routine of strenuous physical exercise by the information in the preceding two chapters, you are ready to visualize putting yourself on Maharam's Curve. You are about to sense for yourself how
strongly the psychological approach used in Maharam's
Curve correlates with the concrete advantages of exercise. At
the same time, don't forget the image of equilibrium I have
discussed before, the circle that balances all factors in our
program, from taking a positive attitude to eating smart,
from warming up for an exercise session to buying the right
sports equipment.

In this chapter I want you to see the overall shape of the
Curve at work: Phases I, II, and III. In the following three
chapters I'll discuss each phase separately, giving more advice and examples specific to each phase.

The best introduction to the specifics is to spend a few
moments looking over the graph below and carefully reading
the following discussion. The scale on the left is used to indicate mood. Based upon the mood scale explained in Chapter
Four, you will see that zero represents a neutral mood. I've

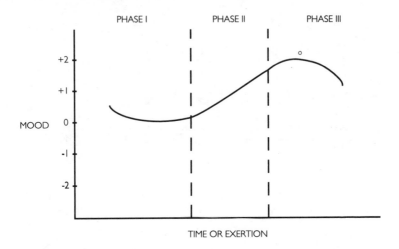

set the neutral mood point (or mood level zero) about half-way up the scale.

To give an overview of a successfully achieved program, I've used the bottom scale to represent time, but only in a very general way. Phase I, for example, takes about two to three weeks for most people. During this initial period, as you can see from the nearly straight line, the mood levels of most people will not change noticeably.

Most of my patients have no problems, either physical or psychological, during Phase I, even though the benefits of the Curve are not yet appearing. Occasionally, though, someone has to be encouraged to continue. The 31-year-old mother of a newborn and a 2-year-old came to me because she wanted to lose weight gained during her pregnancy, but she found that she had no time for regular exercise. After a week or so of trying to get into Phase I, she was not sure she could continue. I suggested she find a group of mothers in similar situations so that they could take turns babysitting each other's children. There was no such group in her suburban New Jersey neighborhood, so she organized one. She was soon working through Phase I toward Phase II.

Beginners are probably most vulnerable during Phase I,

since they have not yet experienced the fun of exercise. They are also more likely than veteran exercisers to have unrealistic expectations of dramatic overnight change.

After two weeks of serious effort, Cheryl, a medical assistant in her thirties, was ready to quit.

"I'm not enjoying this at all," she moaned. A couple of questions revealed that she was also sadly disappointed that she could not yet see any results in the mirror. A beginner at regular exercise, she imagined herself to be grotesquely overweight and had expected to see the pounds melt away in front of her eyes.

"I'm not changing fast enough," she explained.

This was a case where I could rely upon friendly persuasion. "Try to trust me," I said. "I promise you there is light at the end of the tunnel." She agreed to try. By the end of the fourth week, she was a believer.

That moment, in fact, is the beginning of Phase II—the moment when you suddenly discover that Maharam's Curve does indeed work for you. If you look back at the graph on page   , you'll see the mood levels beginning to rise. As with Phase I, there is no specific length assigned on the graph to Phase II; the extent of this phase, also, is going to depend on your individual experience. It is likely to be much briefer than the first phase, however, and it will certainly be much more fun. If you were already exercising regularly beforehand, you probably zipped right through Phase I and will not need long to work your way through Phase II. It is a time for learning about the feelings of elation that you have probably experienced during exercise sessions before, but without knowing how to think about them.

Beginners usually find Phase II to be one exciting discovery after another, once they get used to the idea that strenuous exercise really does have something to do with feeling good. Without knowing it consciously, perhaps, the beginner has to fight that old (and perniciously silly) misconception: "No pain, no gain." The word should be "effort," not "pain." No effort, no gain. You have to make the effort, sure, but in Phase II you will enjoy the great pleasure of watching your mood levels and learning for yourself how your exercise program affects them.

"I'm doing it! I'm doing it!" a graphics artist practically shouted into my ear on the telephone. For this 54-year-old woman who had never exercised regularly, Phase II was hitting her stride on long walks in the park. She felt younger, the tedious little projects that sometimes came her way did not get her down as they used to, and she firmly believed that her artistic skills had gained in definition.

In my experience, no one who sticks to a regular exercise program—beginner or veteran exerciser—has failed to get on the Curve. Every time someone has seemed to fail, it's turned out to be a false alarm.

Jeff, a 19-year-old college student who had youth and athletic ability on his side, was stuck in Phase I for several weeks, and I began to wonder. He came to my office weekly with a hang-dog air; gradually, certain salient facts began to emerge. He couldn't answer some of my questions because he wasn't doing his mood scale on a regular basis. And that failure was in part caused by the hangovers he was earning at fraternity parties; he was a champion beer guzzler.

I was dumbfounded when I found out about all this. "It's your choice," I told him. "But it seems to me you're wasting your time and money coming to this office. This world-class drinking is undermining your whole program." Jeff, I'm afraid, did not have much of a response and did not return, so I can only assume that the hops won out.

After Phase I and Phase II, you are going to learn to fine-tune your own personal program in Phase III. Once again, look back at the graph on page 88 and note how Maharam's Curve becomes bell-shaped in this final phase. At the top of the Curve, at a point that is yours alone, you have found the magic point of elation that is your maximum possible high.

While you are getting used to that concept, let me add some reinforcement by way of sex, in a manner of speaking. A psychologist friend recommended me recently to one of his patients, a bright, sensitive, 35-year-old woman who was seriously depressed. A homemaker who was bored with housework, she had let herself get out of shape, and she complained, not surprisingly, that her sex life was "the pits." Like many psychologists today, my friend has found that appropriate exercise can sometimes help lift the spirits of mildly depressed people. He was aware of an Arizona State University study that showed that anywhere from 6 to 90 minutes of aerobic activity will lift the spirits. He hoped I would simply propose a schedule of exercises.

Please recall my earlier warnings that I am not practicing psychiatry. On the other hand, anyone interested in exercise has to recognize the psychological component. For example, you don't need to be a psychiatrist to know that a person who is afraid of exercise or who, conversely, exercises to the point of pain has an unexpressed psychological need. There is a strong psychological component in the manner in which many of us approach exercise, whether it's to make a radical change in our lives or to forget our troubles.

Moreover, it is worth noting that several studies have concluded that regular running can be almost as effective as psychotherapy in treating depression that is mild to moderate. There is a correlation between lower aerobic capacity and levels of depression, between decreased subjective anxiety and exercise. One therapist felt that an upper limit of 20 miles of running per week, combined with traditional treatment, was of maximum benefit to his patients.

In this case, my psychiatrist friend expected that exercise could supplement his own program of treatment, in the same ways suggested by these studies. He was unaware of my work developing Maharam's Curve, but I had already become convinced of the message of this book: it's almost always a mistake to introduce someone to a new exercise program without showing him how to get on the Curve. And it's probably doubly or triply a mistake with a depressed patient, who by definition needs the affirmation of increased mood levels.

Mary, as I'll call her, was cooperative, if not enthusiastic, from the beginning. She was ready to try anything, I suppose, and she agreed to start running three times a week. Working together, we built her pace gradually. As I recall, it took her about five weeks to become aerobic or, in other words, to reach a mood level of + 1.5 with consistency. That means that she had worked her way through Phase I of Maharam's Curve. (If it will help you, look back at the illustration of the Curve as I describe her progress.) For the following three weeks, she stayed in Phase II, carefully charting her mood levels and learning how to enjoy life again. At the beginning of the program, the cards showed that she woke up in a negative mood every morning. Toward the end of Phase I, she always woke up at mood level zero. On exercise days, she could depend upon her run to bring her to higher levels. And her sex life became good again.

How will you get there yourself, to the optimum mood levels, the possible peak experiences, and the innumerable benefits of consistently enjoyable exercise?

For the next three chapters, I am going to go through the program step by step. For you, as for the patients I've mentioned before, learning the Curve is going to be easy, fun, and exciting, with a few surprises along the way.

Up to now we've looked at the overall shape and theory of Maharam's Curve and glanced at the three phases. That should give you the overall picture. Next we are going to go through each of those phases, one chapter at a time. (You might want to look back at this chapter occasionally, in order to remind yourself how a phase fits into the whole program.)

Let's get on with it!

GETTING ON THE CURVE: PHASE I

> People who turn fitness and sports into a fun activity are the ones who end up doing it the rest of [their] lives.
>
> —Arnold Schwarzenegger

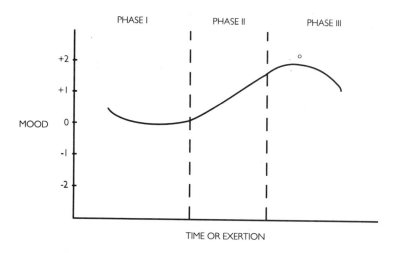

As you've already seen, getting on the Curve—that is, finding your own personal Maharam's Curve—is a three-stage process. In the next three chapters, we'll see how the average person moves through Phases I, II, and III.

Phase I: Taking It Easy

Beginners will go more slowly through this phase, but everyone, no matter how experienced, should take the same series of simple steps to get on the Curve. If you are the kind of exerciser who believes in going for "the burn," think again. That kind of overexertion can be counterproductive physically and mentally. No one has ever turned into Mr. or Ms. America overnight, but I suspect that millions of Americans have tried. They have plunged too precipitously into exercise without adequate preparation and have suffered the kind of pain that defeats the whole purpose of physical fitness.

Our initial goal is going to be the minimum program for the exercise high: a gradual working up to three 20-minute training sessions each week. For many years, this schedule was thought to be the absolute minimum for getting the benefits of aerobic training, for pushing the heart to its target rate. According to very recent research, you can earn many of the aerobic benefits of regular exercise by training only 10 minutes three times a week, but you will not be able to find and maintain the optimum position on your personal Maharam's Curve. Moreover, the American College of Sports Medicine (ACSM) still recommends the more extended periods of exercise for healthy adults:

ACSM GUIDELINES

1. Train three to five days a week.
2. Work out at 60 to 90 percent of maximum heart rate, or 50 to 85 percent of $\dot{V}o2$ max, the maximum rate of oxygen intake.
3. Exercise aerobically for 20 to 60 continuous minutes.

4. The activity can be anything that uses large muscle groups and is rhythmical and aerobic in nature, such as walking, hiking, running, cycling, cross-country skiing, dancing, rope jumping, rowing, stair climbing, swimming, skating, and various endurance game activities.

So push on for that additional 10 minutes so that you can follow the program.

(Experienced exercisers need only glance over the information in this chapter. You have, in effect, been exercising in Phase I all along and are probably ready to move on to Phase II.)

Getting into Phase I

1. *Don't rush it.* If you do too much, or go too fast, you'll lose interest.

2. *Shoot for the neutral mood.* At the end of each exercise session, do your mood scale. If you are a beginner, you are unlikely to rise above the neutral mood for the first two to four weeks of the program. If you already exercise regularly, you should begin moving up the Curve more rapidly.

3. *Stop if you get negative feelings.* You'll know that you're exercising too much, doing something wrong, or working against some unacknowledged obstacle when your mood drops into negative numbers.

For beginners, this is the danger point, because you will not be getting any benefit, and the negative mood will just reinforce any resistance you feel to exercise.

Add variety by alternating easy sessions with hard workouts, or a full week at half-speed with a week at full throttle. Joan Benoit Samuelson, the Olympic marathon runner, alters her distances and paces in training and also incorporates alternative sports and exercise.

4. *Follow the 20 percent rule.* Dr. John McNerney advises,

and I agree, that you should "Never increase your exercise program from week to week more than 20 percent." If you run a total of 30 miles in your three sessions this week, for example, you shouldn't add more than 6 miles (20 percent, or ⅕, of 30 miles) to your total next week.

In terms of Maharam's Curve, Dr. McNerney's rule helps avoid the kind of negative mood drops that discourage exercise. Generally speaking, there's no reason to increase your exercise level if you're feeling good.

5. *To establish your pace*, you can use a simple metronome, the kind music students use during practice. It is generally a triangular-shaped wooden device with a pendulum that can be set to swing back and forth at a set pace, helping the musician maintain a steady and appropriate beat. (Electronic versions also exist today.) Find a piece of music that gives you your correct pace, adjust the metronome until it clicks in time with the music, and it will give you a beats-per-minute pace. If your chosen song is a version of "Granada" played rather slowly, the metronome may show a 60-beats-per-minute pace. You can use that number wherever you exercise by occasionally referring to your wristwatch as you work out.

Of course, you don't have to get hung up on using a metronome to find a pace. You can use an 8-minute mile as a pace, say, or 20 minutes in your target heart range. Or exercise to your Walkman, finding the pace of the song you choose by checking against the second hand of your wristwatch and noting it in your diary. When you want to raise your pace, choose a slightly faster song on one of your cassettes, find the pace, and note that down in your diary. You don't want to make huge leaps from 60 beats per minute to 100 beats per minute, but, if you listen to your body, you can increase the pace sensibly and gradually.

By using the Walkman, you can think of the music as you work out, not the number . . . which is much more fun. You can, by the way, check the exercise magazines for audiocassettes specifically recorded to help you maintain your individual pace. In some product lines, an entire tape has a single, unvarying pace. In others, each tape will have a variety of songs, giving you a wide range of choices of beats per minute (bpm).

Warning: For the work we are doing, you will only use one song—one pace—at a time.

As you concentrate on the physical work of Phase I, you should also pay attention to the mental resources that can help you make your way to Phase II.

Getting over the Hump: Aids that Work

As long-distance runners and other serious athletes know, one vitally important mental tool is "visualization." Some champions believe in sitting down alone in a quiet room, closing their eyes, and rehearsing every move they intend to make in a downhill ski run or 100-meter hurdles. To runners, the ultra-marathoner Tarak Kauff advises, "Imagine that you are simply the pilot, sitting back, guiding your feet, while another self, with limitless energy, is running the race through you. . . . Just think that you are along for the ride."

Connie Paraskevin-Young, the world champion sprint cyclist, is even more specific in her visualizing: "I picture everything that's there—where those flagpoles are, where those stands are, where my bike pit area is, who I'm going to be competing against—in as much detail as possible. I visualize myself racing . . . going through the moves and going through them properly."

In *Peak Performance*, world-class weightlifter Dr. Charles Garfield describes his discovery of his own mind-body connection when working with Eastern European sports scientists. At the time, he could bench press 280 pounds and expected to reach a goal of pressing 365 pounds after a year of rigorous training. His colleagues, however, had a surprise for him. They encouraged him to try various techniques of mental preparation—deep muscle relaxation, self-psyching, and visualizing. Within mere minutes, Dr. Garfield was pressing 300 pounds. Less than an hour afterward, as he continued to experiment with these techniques, he had reached his goal of 365 pounds.

The concept of visualizing that Dr. Garfield used is, in particular, increasingly popular as a performance-enhancing technique among amateur and professional athletes who recognize the importance of the mind-body connection. Before even taking the ski lift, a downhill skier might pause and concentrate on recalling the best run she has ever made. To help imprint the memory, she will focus specifically on the physical and emotional sensations of that day—weather, condition of the snow, time of day, sounds at the heights, dryness or moisture in the air, clothes she was wearing . . . whatever will bring back that personal best when she actually hits the slopes. The trick is to focus on the positive. A tennis player, say, will replay his best match, feeling the sensation of making an ace or recalling the instant at which he made an incredible save. Before winning the U.S. Open, Gabriela Sabatini visualized the game she knew she had to play: "I pictured rushing the net and fighting for each point."

According to sports psychologist Kay Porter, Ph.D., who coauthored *Visual Athletics,* many high-performance athletes practice visualization quite naturally, playing out the upcoming game or exercise like a movie in their head and encouraging themselves to do their best. As Dr. Porter explains, "You are, in a sense, reprogramming your subconscious mind." She has compiled a list of instructions to help athletes and exercisers boost their performance by using visualization:

DR. KAY PORTER'S STEPS TO VISUALIZATION

1. See, hear, and feel yourself performing your event.
2. Write down all the details.
3. Begin when you arrive and continue while you are warming up.
4. Go into detail; include the weather, sights, smells, sounds, and positive feelings.
5. Imagine yourself relaxed, confident, powerful, and in control of your body and mind. Include positive statements about your success and key words you can call on during your real performance.
6. Go through your whole event, thinking of each significant part. Feel yourself moving smoothly with strength and endurance.
7. Write statements about relaxation; remind yourself you have confidence, power, and mental toughness.
8. Reread your notes and edit them into a script. Dictate your script into a tape recorder.
9. Listen for flaws or points that you can improve, and rerecord the script.
10. Listen to your tape at least three or four times a week while you're in a quiet, relaxed environment.

But many people need help in learning how to visualize. They can benefit from a technique known as NLP (neurolinguistic programming), a fairly recent psychological tool that can work wonders for athletic performance. For example, at the medical booth of the New York City Marathon, insecure runners often seek advice from medical coordinator Yolanda Rodriguez, who introduced the use of teams of psychologists at the annual event.

"Look directly at me," she says softly to a worried runner. "Now, close your eyes and concentrate on seeing yourself. . . . Do you see yourself yet?" When the runner nods, Yolanda asks, "Do you feel good?" "Yes." "Good," she says,

"I want you to hold that feeling. . . ." As the runner concentrates, she touches his shoulder, "anchoring" the good feeling as a way of instilling confidence for the race ahead. Almost without fail, the runners who spend these few moments with Yolanda return after the marathon to thank her for helping them do their best on the course. NLP is used in treatment of many different kinds of psychological problems, from schizophrenia to addiction; the version used in athletics is not treatment but affirmation. With the help of another person, you can visualize your physical goals, then link them with positive mood by "anchoring." As you exercise or participate in your sport, you recall that touch on the shoulder, and the combination of precise image and good feelings will come back in a rush.

For my patients, I suggest a kind of do-it-yourself "anchoring" before exercise sessions. I advise them to sit in a comfortable chair, close their eyes, breathe deeply, and picture themselves actively performing *and enjoying* their chosen exercise. When the feeling of enjoyment is strong, they can "anchor" it by gripping the arms of the chair for a moment, imprinting that good feeling. Immediately afterward, they should open their eyes, get out of the chair, and start exercising!

Visualization works for athletes or exercisers at any level of achievement, but with one proviso: you have to be realistic about your goals. Visualizing yourself running a marathon when you haven't worked out in several years is just asking for negative reinforcement. You must define a realizable goal, then visualize yourself achieving it. Jackie Joyner-Kersee, the 1988 Olympic gold medalist whom sportswriters like to call the "world's greatest female athlete," believes so strongly in the value of visualization that she uses it for everything from preparing for her championship performances in the heptathlon to walking in high heels: "I'm afraid of falling, so I visualize myself walking perfectly."

Going Slow

If you are exercising for the first time, you will have to start out cautiously. Visualize your first few laps around the track or your first few minutes on the exercise bike. Also, think about your motives for exercise. Want to lose weight? Visualize yourself in slightly trimmer clothing, catching your reflection in a shop window. Want to have greater stamina for a hike in the mountains? Visualize yourself creasting the top of a ridge, coming upon a panorama that stretches far into the distance. Want to feel more zest in the bedroom? Well . . .

If you can begin to see yourself in the mind's eye as a performer who has grace, speed, and agility, you will be even more strongly motivated to become that kind of performer in reality. Also, according to professional athletes, the practice of visualizing your next exercise session or athletic contest can sometimes alert you to potential pitfalls. "After a certain point," according to a player for the Boston Bruins, "the game is all mental." Elizabeth Manley, silver medalist in figure skating at the 1988 Winter Olympics, says that she spent almost as much time on mind as on body in the year before the competition. "I had always had the techinique; I had the motivation; but without my sports psychologist, I wouldn't have had the performance." She learned to visualize herself performing the most technically demanding jumps with aplomb and skating with confidence through her whole routine.

In running, imagine yourself plying the actual course, visualizing the surroundings as clearly as possible and associating them with a good, positive mood. If you are not yet familiar with your course, you should visualize having good feelings as you run down the two blocks you can see immediately ahead of you, or the wide bend around the reservoir that is open to your view. Eventually, when you get to know the course, you can visualize your run from beginning to end, linking specific points along the way with feelings you want to have as you pass them. If you always feel fatigue at a certain point, visualize that point and imagine a sudden surge of energy and self-confidence. Whatever the sport or type of exercise, you want to play back the whole experience in your mind, "anchoring" the good parts and coming up with mental encouragement for the usual rough spots. "At the thirteenth mile, I know I'll begin to get tired," says Lisa Watts, a recreational marathoner who lives in Boston, "so I picture the end of the run with my husband and all my friends rooting for me. I see myself running easily, looking good, and feeling strong. And it works."

Along with visualization during Phase I, you might want to play various other tricks on yourself, always in the interest of avoiding negative moods and reaching for higher mood levels.

Choose a setting that gives you some visual distraction—anything from a scenic path beside a sparkling reservoir to the changing images of MTV. Think of lessening the potential strain on your body: a dirt track is much easier on your feet, joints, and ligaments than asphalt is. You might even award yourself prizes for sticking to your exercise program: something new to wear to go with your changing self-image. Take along music or the news or a spoken novel on your Walkman if that helps carry you forward, or make sure that you exercise with a friend whose company makes the effort that much lighter.

Above all, remember that *Phase I is not working for you if it becomes an ordeal.* If you are in pain, check back over these past few chapters to see whether or not you're breaking one of the basic rules. Are you overdoing it? Did you neglect to get a physical? Could you be using equipment that is inappropriate or ill-fitting for your chosen exercise?

Recently, a patient who had been in Phase I for only a couple of weeks told me, rather matter-of-factly, that she was feeling throbbing pain from her waist down to her heels the day after each exercise session. Despite everything I'd said, she just assumed that exercise does this to you. It didn't take long to discover that she was never taking the time to stretch before or after her workouts.

Sometimes my evaluations of my patients deal with a different kind of issue—psychological resistance to change. One very athletic young woman who claimed to love running presented me with an unusual problem: Sherry had to give up running because she liked TV soap operas so much she couldn't bear to miss them. At the same time, she felt physically out of sorts because she wasn't getting any strenuous exercise on a regular basis. Naturally, I suggested she set her VCR to record these daytime dramas while she ran, but Sherry felt her schedule was too tight to view them later. She got home from work just in time for her programs; afterward, she began cooking dinner for her family, and she wanted to spend the rest of the evening with them. Well, then, I thought, why not set up a stationary bicycle in front of the TV screen and exercise at home while the soaps were sudsing? This proved to be the answer for getting Sherry into Phase I.

Someone else who had no free time to begin Phase I was Arnold M., an ambitious junior partner in a Wall Street law firm. Every available moment had to go to the company, he believed. This paunchy 33-year-old had never exercised before, but he recognized that physical fitness was essential. We had long talks about finding a way to focus on essentials, on prioritizing various aspects of his life. Finally, I realized something from his conversation.

"Listen, Arnold," I said, "you seem to have long-range and short-range goals with your company. Why not do the same thing with me? I'll give you a short-range goal: say, in about six weeks after you start exercising regularly, you'll notice an improvement in your mood. And we'll take a long-range goal of exercising regularly for at least three months, no matter what."

Arnold M. agreed. After six weeks he realized that he was happier and more productive, and after three months he was set to exercise on Maharam's Curve for the rest of his life. Ironically, by setting aside the time to exercise, he found that he needed to spend less time in the office. Before exercising, Arnold had been getting to his desk an hour-and-a-half early each business day. But once he was on the Curve, he was able to cut back to 45 minutes, because he felt he was that much more efficient in his work.

I'll say it again: the aim of Maharam's Curve is to teach exercisers how to maximize their enjoyment of workouts and to help them develop the natural human desire to exercise frequently. To me, that aim does not include the endurance of unnecessary pain.

For review, consider these seven basic principles for cardiovascular training:

SEVEN BASIC CARDIOVASCULAR TRAINING RULES FOR RIDING MAHARAM'S CURVE

1. Your heart is a muscle. To strengthen it, you must exercise.
2. Not only must you bring your pulse rate into your individual training range, you must also maintain that rate without interruption.
3. You must exercise a minumum of 20 minutes three times a week for cardiovascular fitness on the Curve. More (but not too much) will increase the beneficial effects of exercise.
4. Your pulse rate must not fall below your training range during the exercise session.
5. The type of exercise is unimportant as long as you get the properly strenuous workout.

6. A new exercise program should begin gradually. For the first week or two, don't struggle to maintain your training range for the entire 20 minutes.

7. As you train over a period of time, your heart will strengthen and your natural pulse will drop because the heart muscle will pump more efficiently. To maintain the benefits of your exercise, you will have to exercise harder.

Now you are prepared to begin Phase I: you know how to use the mood scale; you know the target heart range you have to aim for; and you will try to keep in mind at all times, as an ideal goal, the circle of equilibrium that represents the proper balance of mind and body.

Plotting Your Own Curve—Phase I

You need at least two weeks of aerobic exercise under your belt (remember, for our purposes, that's three 20-minute sessions per week) before it makes sense to begin to plot your own Curve. Even if you have been exercising regularly, it probably makes sense to wait, because you are adjusting to a new way of thinking about your exercise.

Let's say that your diary looks something like the one shown on page 106:

Using this information, you can make your own graph, following the general idea of the graph on page 107 but adding the specifics of your own exercise program. Remember, you are plotting your own personal Maharam's Curve, not trying to align your moods with a model Curve.

For each date on which you exercise, this graph (see page 107) will show your mood level, which you determine *after* your workout, and the pace you reached in that session.

At this point, you are trying to establish a mood pattern that rises consistently above the bar sketched above at

SAMPLE DIARY PAGE NO. 3

DATE	MOOD		PACE
1	+ ½		
2	+ ¾		
3	+ ½		
4	+ ¾		
5	+ 1		

Note: Pace must stay consistent at this time. Record it so that you can refer to it at a later time.

mood level zero. When that happens, you will be on the Curve. In fact, you will have moved on to Phase II.

It doesn't matter what standard you use for your pace, so long as you use it consistently. It can be the number of miles you run in a session, or the heart rate you sustain throughout your workout. If you are using the kind of exercise machine that shows the number of calories consumed per hour, use that figure as your pace.

Just as a reminder, here's the schedule you follow for each exercise session: You warm up, you stretch, you exercise aerobically (within your target heart range) for at least 20 minutes, you warm down, you stretch, you do your mood scale, you use some standard as a pace—and you write down your mood and pace on your graph. If you are exercising to music and change your songs, you always check with the

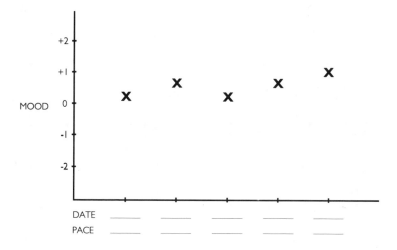

DATE   _____   _____   _____   _____   _____

PACE   _____   _____   _____   _____   _____

metronome for the change in pace and make a note of it.

As you continue to keep this record, you will notice that your mood levels are gradually rising, after an initial flat period. (Any exception, whenever your mood drops, is still something to worry about, even after you have been on the Curve a while, just as in the beginning of the program.) As the curve swings upward toward the right, the day will come when the truth is unmistakable: after all of your preparation and hard work, after your use of the mood scale and your record-keeping, your will recognize that your moods are elevated and you are actually riding Maharam's Curve!

PLOTTING YOUR CURVE: PHASE II

I feel like a million dollars.

—Lorrin ''Whitey'' Harrison,
78-year-old recuperating from quintuple bypass surgery
by surfing in the Pacific Ocean

The transition from Phase I to Phase II is as individual as every other aspect of Maharam's Curve.

Only you can tell when you've crossed the line . . . and the recognition will probably come after the fact. One day you will realize that you have been consistently keeping your mood above neutral for two or three weeks.

That's it.

No bells clanged, no lightning struck. It's much better than that. You just gradually slip into a pattern of ongoing physical and psychological well-being. You don't feel hassled or exhausted. You don't necessarily feel exhilarated, but you do feel balanced. For many people, this achievement of mind and body equilibrium is so natural that they hardly recognize the change. That's as it should be. This is the state you *should* enjoy as a normally active human being. This is where your mind and body want to be for the rest of your life.

Remember my highly motivated patient, the lady with the fur coat? Like many goal-oriented people, she didn't recognize her own Phase II at first.

After a few weeks of her program, she called me in some disgust.

"Doctor, it's not working for me. This is going nowhere."

"Wait a minute," I said. "Are you feeling good these days?"

"Well, sure."

"Elevated . . . ?

There was the pause during which light dawns.

"That's it?"

"That's it!"

And it is. As a reader, if you've started a program, you might be saying, "So I've been feeling good. That's it? That's why I bought this book?"

Yes, that's it. You have crossed the line to Phase II, and now you have to pause a while and spend time recognizing what you've achieved. As I have noted previously, experienced exercisers may well want to move ahead of other readers, but only with due caution.

For example, when a 25-year-old playwright who had been running regularly for ten years came to me, his mood profiles were consistently +1. He had in essence already reached Phase II on his own. Even so, I suggested he stay there for another two weeks and practice learning to use the cards and the mood and pace diary. Theoretically, I suppose, he was ready for Phase III, but some extra practice would make plotting his moods routine and free him to concentrate on fine-tuning his Curve.

If you are an experienced exerciser who is already in Phase II, you can decide for yourself when to try to move on. I would err on the side of caution. If you've been exercising for years, you can wait another couple of weeks before getting into Phase III. Deferred gratification never hurt anyone.

As for readers who are unused to exercise, caution and a steady rate of development are even more critical. Another of my very hard-working patients, a Wall Street attorney, leaped on the program like gangbusters. Even though he had never found exercise enjoyable, he wanted the health benefits. In my office, he took copious notes; at home, he assiduously did the cards. In the beginning, his mood tended to hover around neutral. After about four weeks, he was averaging +1.

He too phoned to say that he wasn't getting anywhere in terms of Maharam's Curve.

"You know, Doc, I'm doing everything you said. I'm running, I get up to my maximum heart rate at least twenty minutes three times a week, I'm doing the mood scale, but nothing's happening. I mean, when do I get the 'high'?"

"You've been plus-one for the last two weeks. That's it!"

"Oh, no. I don't feel high."

"Okay. But your mood is elevated after each exercise session. You haven't had an 'explosive' high, but you are always above mood zero. Tell me, how do you feel about exercise now?"

"Well, I have to do it. I feel bad when I don't."

"That's it. You're in Phase II."

Characteristically, this particular patient didn't really believe he was on the Curve until he went back to his notebook and looked at his record of his mood scales. Once he believed his statistics, he was able to believe his own feelings. About two weeks later, following my advice to hang loose for a while and become familiar with his +1 feelings, he called to say he was ready to go on to Phase III.

"I'm eager to find my peak," he said. His timing was absolutely right. Don't expect to be ready for that goal until you too learn to achieve, sustain, and enjoy the elevated moods of Phase II. They are the necessary foundation for learning to rise on the Curve.

So don't let the elevated moods of Phase II slip away just because you don't recognize them for what they are . . . and don't get pumped up to rush on to the next phase of the Curve. The first goal of Phase II is to spend a couple of weeks "hanging out," reveling in the new feelings, learning to recognize and recall them. The mood elevation you've reached may seem strangely familiar, because you may have experienced it briefly during exercise in the past. Now you have to learn to savor it so that you can take control of it. Don't rush. Try to understand that your elevated mood ebbs and flows. Have fun. After all, that's the point of the whole program.

A 37-year-old homemaker just couldn't wait, and she even suspected my motives for advising her to hold back. After only two exercise periods that brought her up to + 1 or a bit more, she announced that she wanted to try for Phase III.

"But you've had mood elevation for only about four days all told," I warned. "You haven't had time to enjoy the experience and learn how it works for you."

She set her jaw. "You're milking me!"

(Here in New York, that's called "straight talk.")

"I'm doing no such thing. I'm trying to make the program work for you. If you're determined, I'll certainly tell you how to go on to Phase III, but I urge you not to do it. You're not aerobically trained yet. Your body and your mind are not ready."

She was insistent, so I sketched out the information you will read in the next chapter. A week later, she called to report that she was feeling negative moods after each exercise session. This was to be expected. She'd leaped ahead too quickly. I took her back to Phase I and let her work up to Phase II again. She stayed there about four weeks, building a solid aerobics base. During this period of sensibly gradual development, in fact, she experienced an "explosion." In the end, she would be well prepared for the fine-tuning of Phase III.

Examples of Phase II

For some people, the definitive Phase II feeling is simply an increased peacefulness, but it lies above the neutral mood on the scale. Others may feel euphoria. Whatever the elevated feeling, it has to be understood before you can go on to Phase III.

As I've noted earlier, Phase II hits many people with a big rush. Others seem to resist it right up to the end, as if unwilling to believe that something so powerful could happen with so little fanfare. It was one of the "gain-through-pain" people, a 27-year-old MBA, who took the longest of anyone I've known to recognize the obvious. A meticulous accountant who loved to work in his office on weekends, George hadn't been able to move out of Phase I after six weeks of trying— and he knew why.

"Your program isn't intense enough," he said. To compensate, he was doing his mood scale at all times of day and

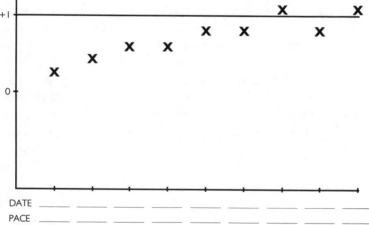

YOUR CURVE DURING PHASE II

night, closely charting his every fluctuation in feeling. This was a mistake in focus, it seemed to me.

"Look, George," I suggested, "stop trying to outthink the Curve, because that's what you're doing."

"Well," he said, "I do think about my mood all the time I'm running."

"Exactly. Let it just happen."

He did, and it did.

My advice to George applies to everyone who has reached Phase II. Don't think too much about what's happening to you. Simply enjoy the good feelings. Don't fiddle around with your exercise pace, so long as you continue to reach your target heart range throughout each workout. Just remain consistent and enjoy!

Phase II, in fact, is when beginners recognize at last that all the rest of us who have been exercising for years are not lunatics. We knew something after all! Even veteran exercisers have to share in the delight of people who are having this revelation for the first time.

"Thanks, Doc, for making me do it," an account executive at an advertising agency said to me. After four weeks of Phase I, he had reported that he didn't feel even a twinge of pleasure, but he stubbornly persisted because he had seen others suddenly fly into Phase II. In his case, though, as has happened with several of my patients, his wife and his boss seemed to recognize that he was on the Curve before he did. "You're in a foul mood," his wife began saying. "Go out and run. That always makes you easier to live with." His boss began complimenting him: "Hey, you sure are sharper than usual today." Finally, the account exec caught on. He was not only feeling better, but he began to have a whirlwind of creative ideas while he was out running. He had made the transition to Phase II.

Heightened creativity was also the unexpected extra benefit for an overweight nightclub comic who came to me for help in devising a program that would get his weight down.

His running program didn't do much about that problem, but it did help his act, or so he claimed. Once he slipped into Phase II, he told me, the jokes came flying as he ran. And TV actress Joan Van Ark tells me that she finds she can hone her acting skills while running. For example, the right way to approach a difficult scene will suddenly become clear.

When to Move On

In my experience, the average person, whether beginner or experienced exerciser, should have three or four good, solid weeks of the elevated mood plateau of Phase II before even thinking about going on to Phase III.

At this point, not only are your mood levels higher, you should also be feeling more energetic and mentally sharper. Doing your mood levels and pacing should have become a natural part of the routine of your daily life. If you begin to feel the need to exercise more—say, from three sessions weekly to four or five weekly—you could try, but you probably don't need to. The danger is that you may overexercise, slip up and over your peak in Phase III, and start sliding down from that peak, losing your elevated mood levels.

But that danger is slight. For most people who have reached this point in the Curve, there is nothing to fear, everything to look forward to. You have been enjoying— probably with some amazement—the remarkable benefits of pacing yourself on your own personal Curve. You've been having fun. You find that you want to keep exercising regularly. You are beginning to feel some of the wonderful by-products of exercise: greater stamina . . . reduced stress . . . better performance at work and at play . . . increased enjoyment of every aspect of your life.

Why go on to the next phase?

Because now you're going to learn how to take control so that you can adjust your pace and other factors in response to all of the changes you will face in the years to come. Life on the Curve is definitely not static. It is a matter of continual rethinking and readjustment, a constantly exciting exercise of the mind as well as the body. In the next chapter, I discuss the challenges and rewards of the fine-tuning you will learn in Phase III.

PHASE III: FINE-TUNING YOUR CURVE

To go beyond is as wrong as to fall
short.   —Confucius

Now it is time to add to the excitement of Phase II by learning how to reach your optimal mood level, retain it, and regain it virtually at will. In Phase III you will be able to control your pace so that you will predictably achieve optimum mood level, and you will learn to make the adjustments of pace and other factors that will keep your high on your Curve. This is the fine-tuning process.

It is possible that Phase III will also bring you to the rare surge of good feeling I referred to earlier as the "exercise explosion." That peak experience is not possible unless you are at optimum mood level. If it happens, you will recognize it immediately as an incredible burst of physical, mental, and emotional joy. It may happen once and never again, as several of my patients have reported. Some people find that they experience it frequently; some exercisers who achieve optimum mood levels in Phase III for years never experience it. In short, the exercise explosion peak is a wonderful, but occasional, side benefit of Phase III. If it happens, fine; if not, you will still enjoy the lifelong sensation of enjoyable exercise at your optimal mood point on the Curve.

One way of defining that point, or picturing it, is as the fine line between undertraining and overtraining. At your optimal point, you are exercising at peak efficiency—gaining all the long-term physical benefits—and experiencing peak mood levels. Once you've reached that point, your aim is to return to it during each workout . . . but avoid going past it. The secret is to monitor your exercise pace in order to keep your mood at the optimal point.

After three weeks in Phase II, study the record you've been keeping. What is your optimal mood level? This number will not be the same for everyone, so you are not striving to reach a standard goal. Instead, you are simply tracking the apex of your own personal Curve. If you have not reached +2 during your first two weeks of Phase II but are continually bumping against a slightly lower level, that is probably your peak point. If so, you probably feel tired or less elated whenever you try to work past that level.

How to Fine-Tune

To learn to control your exercise so that you can predictably return to your optimal point, you need to know your pace when your mood is at peak. Whether you've been using an 8-minute-mile pace or some other marker, you will find that a specific pace correlates with your most elevated moods. Let's say that your mood scale shows you at your optimal point whenever you've just ridden your bike 10 miles at a particular pace. By now, you are skilled in assessing your moods. It's time to play around. What happens when you bike 12 miles at the same pace? Or if you're at your optimal mood level when you swim at a certain pace (strokes per minute), speed up the pace a bit and see what happens to your mood level. Notice that you *always change only one variable at a time*: that's the key. If you find that your mood increases after a change, then you are still moving up the Curve. If it decreases, you've overreached.

To return to our automobile imagery, fine-tuning the Curve requires the patience and recurring attention of a Jaguar mechanic; the body isn't a pickup truck. Your pace is going to be affected by the diverse physical and emotional factors in your life. When mental stress puts the bite on you, or you've come down with a mild but not disabling infection, your usually reliable pace cannot be expected to bring you up to peak. On a day when you win the lottery, you won't need to run 12 miles to feel exhilarated.

Also, as the months go on and regular exercise becomes a necessary part of your life, your body will become stronger and need greater challenges. The out-of-shape, untrained body has to get the heart pumping to perform well in your first workouts. As you become better trained, you have to exercise harder to make your target heart range and "go aerobic." By the same token, you will have to increase your pace and/or your mileage in order to maintain mood elevation. Remember, even if you have to adjust both pace and mileage, you adjust each one separately; *never* try to change both at the same time.

The Can-Do Compulsive

Like the Type A personality I discussed earlier, another personality stereotype, the "Can-Do Compulsive," has special problems with the challenges of Maharam's Curve—specifically, the thinking required to fine-tune in Phase III.

Simply put, the stereotypical Can-Do Compulsive is goal-oriented, but shortsighted. He concentrates on working long hours in the belief that greater expenditure of effort results in increased productivity. His motto: the longer the work day, the more rapidly you achieve your work goals.

By thinking only about direct cost-benefit, however, he is missing an important aspect of any activity, whether work or play: the indirect cost-benefit that occurs along the way to-ward a goal. In the case of Maharam's Curve, the Can-Do Compulsive runs the risk of missing the day-to-day pleasure of exercise itself and the development of mind and body. Yes, he may well reach an exercise high more quickly than others who take a less single-minded approach, and he may also achieve the physical benefits earlier than most. But this is supposed to be fun!

What the Can-Do Compulsive ignores is that short-term benefits are important, too. The weeks before you attain your high, the sessions after which you feel slight improve-ments in mental attitude or physical well-being—these should be recognized and cherished. By taking note of the short-term benefits, you learn how to expend less energy, to channel your individual efforts toward your long-term goal. Even though the Can-Do Compulsive may get on the Curve faster than the rest of us, he often has a difficult time sum-moning up the patience necessary for introspectively identi-fying mood levels. It would be easier if he could enjoy the present achievement instead of concentrating on future goals.

The Can-Do Compulsive is more prone than others to the dangers of pushing too hard and overtraining. For men, this can result in lower sperm counts and testosterone levels, as well as "sports anemia," marked by weakness, irritability, and fatigue. For women, overtraining can disrupt menstrual cycles, reduce fertility, and diminish bone mass to the point of enhancing the likelihood of osteoporotic fractures. In fact, the incidence of bone and muscle injuries of all types rises precipitously as runners begin to log 30 miles or more each week. Essentially, the first sign of overtraining is deteri-oration in your performance, followed by the symptoms noted above.

In the end, however, the stereotypical Can-Do Compul-sives I have known do not regret that they barreled down the track full-speed ahead. Their goal is to add the knowledge and experience of Maharam's Curve to their belt as fast and as efficiently as possible. That's fine with me, because it's fine with them. But I urge you to pay as much attention to the short-term benefits as to the eventual goal. The mood scale is infinitely easier and more accurate when you can be sensitive to the present moment.

You can continue to be goal-oriented, but add enjoyment of exercise to your list of goals. You can continue to want to excel, but add understanding of emotional needs to your list of desired achievements. You can still view exercise as a means of attaining the specific fitness end you've chosen; at the same time, you should also view raised mood levels as an immediate short-term benefit, an end that is actually part of the means.

Phase III: Don't Resist

One of my patients, an accountant named John C., had a very difficult time learning to adjust his exercise to fit his Curve—obviously not because he couldn't understand the math involved.

He had come to me with one goal only: to get some enjoyment from the exercise he dreaded, but endured because he knew it made him feel healthier and mentally sharper *afterward*. As we worked together, his cards indicated that his moods were gradually elevating and he was consciously aware of these changes. After a couple of weeks on Phase II, he dropped out, claiming, "I don't need those cards any more."

He was mistaken. Six months later, John C. returned to my office, greatly dissatisfied with his exercise. At the time, he was running 14 miles a week at the rate of 8 minutes per mile. His mood had dropped from $+1$ to $+\frac{1}{2}$. He felt the difference, and he was worried. Together we began to adjust his program; in other words, we started the fine-tuning that is essential to Phase III.

First, I suggested he continue his 8-minute-per-mile pace but drop his weekly mileage total to 12 miles. The cards showed that his mood elevated to +1 ½ right away. After a couple of weeks, at my suggestion, he cut back to a total of 10 miles, still maintaining the 8-minute-per-mile pace. Quite soon, his level dropped to +1, indicating that we had decreased his total mileage too much. When he spent a couple of weeks running a total of 12 miles again, his mood rose again to +1 ½. To this point, we had adjusted only one factor in his exercise program.

In most cases, that would have been enough; there is usually no reason to adjust more than one factor, once you find and sustain a peak mood level. In this instance, however, both the patient and I shared an intellectual curiosity about the possible effects of reducing his 8-minute-per-mile pace, which seemed unusually strenuous for an amateur runner in his current physical condition.

I suggested that he slow down to 8 minutes, 20 seconds, per mile for a couple of weeks, but continue to run a total of 12 miles weekly. We were about to strike gold. Almost immediately, the cards showed that the slower pace had elevated John's level to +1 ¾. On the fourth day of the new regimen, he experienced that unusually strong version of the rare exercise high described with such wonder by those who have felt it—the floating feeling, the perfect rhythm, the conviction of being able to go on forever.

Don't Overdo It

Overexercise, even at this point, can put you in the wrong place on the Curve. Ernest, a 47-year-old tax accountant, had been running regularly his entire adult life and was getting bored with the sport. Not only was the thrill gone, but he no longer felt the burst of extra energy after a good workout. On the contrary, he was exhausted. He wanted my advice about choosing a new sport or perhaps giving up altogether.

Ernest's weekly program was three brisk, 15-mile runs. When he followed my advice to do mood scales before, during, and after each of these workouts for a week, it became clear that he was on the down side of Maharam's Curve. Overexercise had pushed him past his optimal point. At my suggestion, he cut his runs by 20 percent to 12 miles each. Ernest tells me that he loves running again and always feels great afterward.

Exhaustion is the most obvious indication of overtraining—or, in our terms, a slide over to the down side of the Curve. Another indication is a 10 percent or larger drop in your average sleep time, or a 10 percent or greater increase in your morning heart rate. Any of these symptoms could suggest that you have crossed the line between undertraining, which provides the body little or no lasting benefits, and overtraining, which is harmful.

John and Ernest became believers, but only after resistance to some of the basic aspects of maintaining optimum placement on Maharam's Curve. Your pathway will be easier if you remember the following four keys to fine-tuning your program during the climactic Phase III.

FOUR KEYS TO FINE-TUNING

1. Adjust only one variable at a time—e.g., pace, distance, time (as on an exercise machine).
2. Keep to the change for at least five exercise periods before trying another adjustment. Assess your mood *immediately* after each session.
3. Average your readings for the five days and compare that average with your previous mood level average.
4. Graph your Curve on graph paper or on the generic

graphs that follow. Remember that your highest point doesn't have to reach + 2; we are all individuals.

Do whatever works for you; this is not to be handed in! Rather, your aim is to work out a chart that accurately documents your moods after each exercise period and reflects the changes in a curve. This is your way of recording exactly what your mind and body are saying to you as you learn how to ride your own personal version of Maharam's Curve.

CHARTING YOUR CURVE

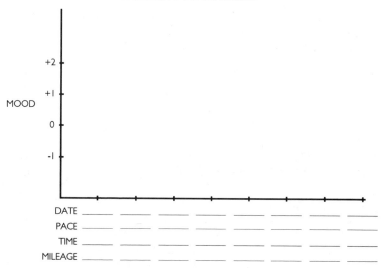

Use whatever unit you choose on the bottom, but be consistent.

CHARTING YOUR CURVE

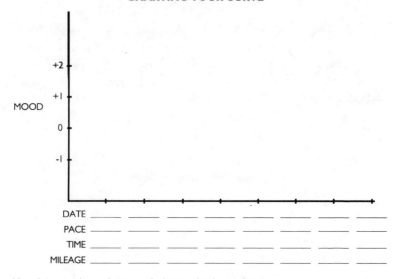

| DATE |
| PACE |
| TIME |
| MILEAGE |

Use whatever unit you choose on the bottom, but be consistent.

CHARTING YOUR CURVE

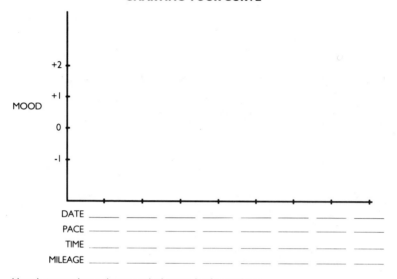

Use whatever unit you choose on the bottom, but be consistent.

CHARTING YOUR CURVE

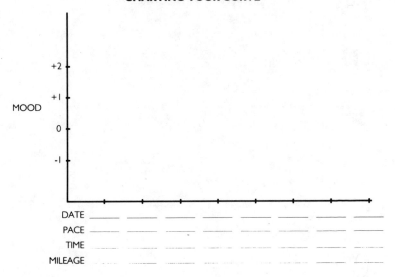

Use whatever unit you choose on the bottom, but be consistent.

CHAPTER ELEVEN

LIFE ON THE CURVE

You are there. Your life has changed. You're feeling healthier and happier. From the day you begin to relax and let yourself enjoy Phase II, you will begin to enjoy the astonishing benefits of life on the Curve. As I discuss later in this chapter, your sex life is bound to be better, you are less likely to let yourself get or stay depressed, you undoubtedly sleep more soundly, and you have more time for your family and friends because you've got more stamina and energy. You're going to live longer. You're going to have more fun in team sports. You're going to be more creative in work and play.

But how does being on the Curve affect your daily schedule? At this point, I always hesitate to give specific examples of your new life on the Curve, because Maharam's Curve can be used with any type of exercise and by exercisers of practically any age or body type. Perhaps you only need to follow the very direct advice of actress Joan Van Ark: "As Nike has so beautifully put it, 'Just do it!'" On the other hand, it might help some readers if I try to suggest, as generally as I can, how you will use the Curve after you have begun the fine-tuning of Phase III.

You get up on a morning that looks like congealed pea soup, and your mood scale shows you feeling − 1. From your record-keeping, you know that 25 minutes on the rowing machine typically brings you from a neutral mood of level zero on the scale to your optimal level . . . and you will be ready and eager to face the day. You get up, "do it," and you're productive even on this day that started out so unpromisingly.

But don't forget one curious failing that most of us share: we find it very easy to slough off a program after the benefits kick in. We don't always practice the virtue of sustaining our efforts. Even though you sail blithely through Phases I, II, and III, your mental abilities improve, and you feel wonderful—you might someday forget how it all came about. Remember: if it worked once, it will continue to work. When things become boring, the fault is in you, not in the Curve. You have to get back on track by rechecking your mood levels, pace, and target heart rate.

One trick is to make a habit of using the language of the Curve. "I'm up one and a half today," a running friend will tell me when she calls. A record producer who regularly runs marathons, she has found that, at least for now, her peak pace is a 7 ½-minute mile. Afterward, her mood almost always rises by that point and a half; if it doesn't, she knows that she has overexerted, so she adjusts her pace the next time.

Perhaps once every ten workouts, by her estimation, she suddenly feels that "explosion," that "floating feeling" that seems to make time stop. Notice that she doesn't adjust her pace in order to recapture that special experience; it will come, occasionally, when everything else falls into place along with her optimal point on the Curve. But she does find, despite all of her experience and her love of the sport, that she has to watch her pace closely. When she doesn't rise 1.5 points, something is wrong.

A slightly less experienced runner, 22-year-old Ron,

found his peak running an 8 ½-minute mile. Three weeks after working into Phase III of the Curve, he felt the "explosion" for the first time. He was startled, because it was as powerful and difficult to describe as all of the literature suggests. That was some time ago, however, and he has never felt it again. Some people never do experience the "explosion."

If you do, fine. The goal of the Curve, as I hope I've made clear, is much more down-to-earth. It helps you find out how to make exercise so enjoyable, so rewarding both physically and mentally, that you will keep exercising from now on. Exercise is demonstrably good for you. Maharam's Curve can help you enjoy what's good for you.

Sex on the Curve

Can Maharam's Curve put the zest back into your love life? I'd bet on it, and recent research tends to back me up, since there is growing evidence that people who exercise feel better about themselves and their bodies—and therefore find renewed joy in sexual activity.

In 1990, for example, a University of California study found that sedentary men who began exercising could improve their sex lives dramatically. On average, the participants attained 75 to 80 percent of their maximum aerobic capacity by working out for an hour about 3.5 days a week. Nine months into the study, they could report that frequency of intercourse had increased by 30 percent, frequency of orgasm by 26 percent. A control group that began a program of mild walking at the same time reported no change or minimal decreases in sexual activity.

Even more startling was the discovery by Bentley College's Phillip Whitten that competitive swimmers have the sex life of men and women 20 to 40 years younger than their actual ages. Surveying a group of swimmers between the ages of 40 and 80, he found, for example, that the swimmers in their forties had sexual intercourse 7.1 times a month on average, while those 60 and over averaged 6.7 times each month.

Enhanced sexual activity and sexual self-image are only two of the predictable benefits of aerobic exercise, but they top the list for many people. In fact, 90 percent of the respondents to a poll conducted recently by the University of South Florida said that their chief reason for exercising was to improve their sex appeal. (Only 30 percent exercised because they wanted to improve their health.) In a similar nationwide study directed solely toward women, 89 percent of the participants said that working out regularly made them feel more confident about their sexuality, while 31 percent reported that, after starting an exercise program, they began making love more frequently.

On the other hand, the concept of balance is as important here as in all aspects of exercise: overtraining can temporarily reduce the sex drive by causing a drop in hormone production. Women athletes can even suffer such exercise-induced hormonal irregularities as amenorrhea, and men who run to the extreme of 200 miles a week will experience a drop in testosterone levels. These problems are caused by exercise excess.

For most people, sensible levels of exercise will produce the good health and good feelings that enhance sexual fulfillment. And forget the stories about sex before a race depriving you of energy. In the first place, even the steamiest sex uses up no more than 100 to 250 calories an hour. The amount you lose in lovemaking the night before a race is less than you will expend in your pre-race warm-up. Second, you should stick to your normal routine before any athletic contest. If you make love at 9:30 P.M. every Friday, you should certainly do so before the big race on Saturday. Sex can relieve the tension that would keep you tossing and turning the night before an important race. But not always. If you usually don't become amorous the night before an important competition, keep Cupid's arrows in the quiver until you've crossed the finish line. Otherwise, your body might feel out of sync.

Just trust the wisdom of Casey Stengel: "It's not the sex that hurts your performance, it's the energy you expend chasing after people to have it with."

The lure of better and more frequent sex may give you just the impetus you need for working your way to your peak on Maharam's Curve.

Out of the Dumps

As I mentioned earlier, researchers have long known that regular exercise can relieve the symptoms of mild and moderate depression. One of the most evident psychological problems of contemporary life, depression can be manifest in many ways: a feeling of impotence, the urge to withdraw from company, inability to "get going" and become active, a generalized feeling of dullness and boredom, loss of sleep, increased anxiety, and decreased ability to concentrate. The dictionary definition sums up what we all recognize as depression: "A great sadness . . . more prolonged than that warranted by any objective reason."

Exercise is certainly not a cure for serious clinical depression. For the kinds of mild and moderate depression that occasionally affect most of us, however, exercise can be an effective antidote.

Some researchers suspect that the benefits result as much from a changed attitude as from the act of exercise itself. In other words, playing a sport that provides relaxation, improved self-confidence, and the enjoyment of using skills will give you a better outlook on life. Many other researchers, however, believe that there is a direct correlation between aerobic exercise and improvements in mood. For example, exercise increases body temperature, thereby promoting better circulation and getting more oxygen to the brain. Is this why moderately depressed feelings dissipate when we exercise? Research into the exact physical or mental causes of the phenomenon continues, but sports medicine physicians agree that, whatever the precise mechanism, alleviation of mild depression is another of the life-enhancing benefits of regular exercise.

Obviously, your work with the mood cards on Maharam's Curve helps you address your depressed feelings directly and effectively. You also can consciously use your exercise pace to maximize the depression-alleviating effects of a workout.

Better for the Heart

Exercise, combined with a decrease in stress and a low-fat diet, can help reduce the blockage in arteries that leads to heart disease. Astonishingly, this combination of factors can even further lessen the risk of cardiovascular disease by shrinking lesions in arteries that are already blocked.

If you are at risk or now suffer from severe coronary heart disease, your physician will recommend the appropriate diet, ways to reduce stress, and a program of exercise. The correct changes in lifestyle can often reverse a dangerous heart condition without the use of surgery or drugs. In a study at the University of California, San Francisco, School of Medicine, more than four out of five patients with coronary heart disease caused by blocked arteries were found to improve after a year of low-fat diet, reduced stress, and regular exercise. Generally, a low-fat diet leads to decreased HDL cholesterol, the beneficial one, as well as the dangerous LDL cholesterol. In this study, LDL was lowered but HDL remained fairly steady. Dean Ornish, M.D., who directed the research, believes that exercise was responsible for maintaining the beneficial HDL levels.

Whatever your physician's recommended program of exercise, it can easily be adjusted to the Curve. In the San Francisco study, for example, patients recovering from heart attacks were advised to take a half-hour walk each day at 50 to 80 percent maximum heart rate, with a day off each week if they wanted. Even within such apparently restricted guidelines, you can vary the pace so as to get your exercise highs on your individual Curve.

Better with the Gang

As you know by now, you cannot get on the Curve by playing a team sport, but the benefits of your exercise program on the Curve will spill over vividly into all of your athletic activities. You will be more productive on the softball field or the volleyball court, at competitive handball or tennis.

As several studies have shown in the case of basketball and tennis pros, an increased aerobic capacity can make you a better team player because your concentration is sharper. You can't be thinking about the strategy of your next play or shot if you're huffing and puffing just to stay up with the game. For another thing, increased stamina developed on the Curve will carry you through unusually lengthy competitive events, a benefit of exercise cited by teenage tennis phenomenon Jennifer Capriati in her own game.

According to Mark Grabow, a conditioning and strength coach in San Francisco, "The secret to having your [basketball] shot go in is to be in shape. The higher your fitness level, then the more consistent your shooting will be throughout a game."

Grabow devised a conditioning plan for one of his clients,

Golden State Warriors basketballer Chris Mullin, that included a daily run or session on a stationary exercise bike, weightlifting, actual basketball games, and catch-and-shoot drills on the court. In the following season, Mullin's average score rose by five points a game. "Once you're in shape," he explained, "you can concentrate on the game. You can also work on making your moves, and you don't have to worry about catching your breath."

Such intensity may not seem immediately related to your weekend pick-up games, but it really is. On the Curve, you will be developing aerobically, increasing your stamina, sharpening your mental and physical skills at the same time, gaining confidence in the use of your body, and reaffirming your love of physical activity.

All of these benefits of regular exercise will become your allies both in team sports and in one-on-one competition.

Sweeter Slumber?

Those who study sleep have solved some of its many mysteries, but many more remain. In connection with exercise, sleep researchers disagree about the probable effects of different levels of exercise upon problems with sleep, but there seems to be a strong consensus that people who exercise regularly *believe* that they sleep better when they exercise than when they don't.

That perception is argument enough for exercise, I think. You don't need laboratory proof when a patient tells you that, after becoming a regular exerciser, she finds that life on the Curve includes waking up feeling more rested than ever before. In my experience, patients who tend to complain about the amount of sleep they get or the quality of their sleep no longer have a problem once they're hooked on exercise. This is not to suggest that exercise is a cure for insomnia, a problem that concerns perhaps a third of us. Medical treatment for insomnia, which is a complex condition, must take into account many different possible factors. For people who have the occasional night of tossing or turning, however, or who wake up vaguely dissatisfied many mornings, exercise may help greatly.

That does not mean exercise in the short run will make much difference, according to some studies; probably the factor that matters most is the fitness that results from regular exercise over a period of time. In other words, if you have never exercised, I don't think a strenuous workout this afternoon is going to waft you into the arms of Morpheus tonight. Rather, you will find that you will begin to sleep better (or think you do) once you have exercised over a long enough period of time to achieve a significantly higher level of fitness. In fact, some experts think that sleep is facilitated only by the kind of high-intensity, aerobic exercise that is basic to your life on the Curve.

Some factors in the exercise/sleep relationship are quantifiable. For example, if sound sleep is an important goal to you, your exercise should be scheduled late in the day, but at least three to four hours before you hit the sack. Why? Apparently, you sleep most easily toward the end of the day, when your body temperature is naturally at its lowest. If you exercise just before going to bed, your body temperature will be elevated too high to allow you to fall asleep immediately with optimum comfort. But if you exercise several hours before your bedtime, thus raising your body temperature with the exertion, your temperature has to rebound, in a sense, to return to its lowest daily temperature. Some researchers believe that this unusually large drop in temperature encourages sleep.

Also, you may be surprised to learn that occasional lack of sleep does not harm your ability to exercise. Although you may feel tired in that situation, your body is prepared with more or less your normal reaction time, endurance level, cardiovascular response, muscle strength, and respiratory response. If you don't exercise because you feel tired, you may be even less likely to sleep well the next night, thus becoming even more fatigued, so that you skip exercise again, and so on and so on until you're really miserable. Of course, when you are feeling the effects of lack of sleep, you should be unusually cautious when you exercise. Decreased mental alertness puts you at increased risk of having an accident or injuring yourself or others.

Better sleep, better sex, a healthier heart, a healthier state of mind, and sharpened skills in team sports—life on the Curve provides extraordinary benefits that money cannot buy and youth may not yet appreciate, and all you have to do is put your mind and body to work.

So it's almost time for you to stop reading and get to work.

Just one last thing: for the exerciser who is not sure which sport is going to be the most helpful, I talk about various popular activities in the next two chapters and show how the Curve applies to each one.

CHAPTER TWELVE

WALKING, RUNNING, RACE WALKING

Get on your feet!   —Gloria Estefan

Just as your Maharam's Curve is as unique to you as your fingerprint, so your exercise prescription will be a matter of personal preference, physical need, scheduling, available facilities, and other factors. In short, an important aspect of maximizing your exercise potential is choosing the sport that is most appropriate to your tastes and circumstances. In this chapter I'll focus on the various advantages, disadvantages, and special Curve techniques of walking, race walking, and running. These are the exercises most commonly chosen by my patients. For many of you, they will form the core of your exercise program from now on, even if you add other activities for physical and mental variety.

How to Choose

The most important factor in your choice of exercise is your enjoyment. You have to sustain your chosen activity throughout Phase I, when the benefits of your Curve have not yet kicked in, and through Phase II, when your results may not yet have become consistently predictable. In other words, you should pick the sport you enjoy for itself, not for its presumed benefits. If you are coming to regular exercise for the first time, and all exercise really does look like a chore despite everything I've said so far, then choose an activity that carries some pleasurable associations or side benefits: running, because you will get to socialize with friends and neighbors; or cycling, because you will get out into the countryside.

This approach is much better in the long run than the Type A approach: trying to choose the sport that offers an ideal of maximum conditioning. Any form of exercise that gets you to your target heart range for 20 minutes three times a week is as good as any other, in purely physical terms, for the goal of reaching Maharam's Curve. Choosing an enjoyable sport is a motivational plus. To help you make regular exercise a part of your life, it is important to maintain a level of enjoyment that brings satisfaction. For the aims of Maharam's Curve, such enjoyment is, of course, essential to learning to attain an exercise high.

Weight loss, however, is the factor that many exercisers like to use as the standard for choosing their activity. If that's your primary motivating impulse, you may want to choose the exercise that is likely to burn the most calories. Turn to Appendix B for a chart highlighting the approximate number of calories burned per hour in sports ranging from football and golf to horseback riding and waterskiing.

Don't just go willy-nilly for the high numbers, however. After you carefully factor in your own vital statistics to determine the number of calories you will expend per hour in a certain sport, consider your potential enjoyment: can you sustain this form of exercise into Phase II and use it consistently to reach your target heart range? For example, a great many amateur swimmers watched Olympic Champion Mark Spitz surging gracefully down the lanes with the butterfly stroke and decided that was an elegant way of swimming aerobically. They tried the same thing and thought they were going to die. The pros can make it look like water ballet, but the butterfly is exhausting.

There is a third variation for choosing your sport. Some exercisers try to select the activity that is least likely to interfere with work or family life or that is most convenient, considering time, expense, location, and other factors.

Certainly, all these considerations are important. An exercise program that disrupts your life, alienates your spouse, or puts you into debt is doomed from the start. I hope my book has made clear that regular exercise is one—and only one—component of complete physical and emotional well-being. Maharam's Curve is a method of maximizing that well-being, not a prescription for a total personality change. It is not a good idea to throw out all the video and audio equipment with one fell swoop and install a home gymnasium instead. Moderation is the key. Development will come at the pace set by your mind and body. Consider the wisdom of this East African proverb: "The best way to eat the elephant standing in your path is to cut it up into little pieces." Glittering new exercise toys are, in themselves, not preferable to a cinder track, a bike, a pool, a flight of stairs. Exercise is supposed to be a fulfilling effort, not conspicuous consumption.

By the way, let me make clear that you are not confining yourself to your first choice of exercise for the rest of your natural days. You will need to stick with it through Phase III, as you adjust your pace to find your peak levels. Changing your form of exercise during the three phases of Maharam's Curve will only confuse the issue and delay your development in my program.

But when you have become expert in riding your Curve and have built up your aerobic capacity and strength, it will be fun to experiment with other types of athletic activity. One of the least helpful attitudes in sports and exercise is the feeling that one activity is so superior that all others have to be denigrated. There simply is no one ideal activity. When you look around, you will find that many kinds of exercise have different, but equivalent, advantages and drawbacks. When you do decide to switch, you must continue to listen to the constant feedback of messages from your body. You will also have to take past injuries into account and keep all of your physical limitations, including age, in perspective.

Now let's look at some of the most popular forms of exercise and see which ones are most appealing to you.

Running and Walking

On the average, this simple formula is accurate: One mile of running or walking in your target heart range will burn off 100 calories. Running just gets you there faster.

For determining fitness levels, however, and to learn to reach your exercise high, you have to think about the length of your exercise period, not the distance you cover. Walking at your target heart range for 20 minutes, even if you cover little more than a mile of ground, is preferable to running three or four miles in 15 minutes.

Be sure you grasp this concept, because it may seem at first glance to fly in the face of common sense. The fleet, lean runner who races to the finish in less than 20 minutes is not raising her own personal fitness level in the manner required by Maharam's Curve. The slower-paced, chubbier walker who stays in his own personal target heart range for 20 minutes three times a week is raising his. Note, too, that anything I say about running or walking applies to the use of a treadmill in the gym or home. The ambiance will not be as various, but the rules of fitness are the same.

Before we compare running and walking in detail, remember that you have to bring your own experience to bear upon your decision. As I've explained before, your goal is to achieve adequate stimulation of the heart and respiratory system. If you have been running regularly, for example, it is unlikely that walking will bring you into the training zone necessary to keep you fit. If you have not been exercising in recent years, leisurely walking may bring you into your target heart range right away. You will probably not be able to sustain this level at a slow pace for very long, however, for your body will snap into shape more rapidly than you probably expect.

Walking

Convenience is the chief advantage of walking. No matter where you go in the world, you can continue your regular schedule of workouts when walking is your exercise of choice. Slow walking is especially effective in improving fitness levels for older, overweight, and/or previously sedentary individuals. It is perfect for anyone with a history of leg or foot injuries. Even low-intensity workouts have been found to reduce the slow walker's risk of heart disease and cancer. "Walking is man's best medicine," wrote Hippocrates.

Because walking is safe for people of any age, sex, or level of fitness, you might assume that you don't have to think about exercise technique. Many of us have developed bad habits over the years, however, so you should take note of the basics:

1. Keep your body relaxed as you walk.
2. Bend your knees slightly and use regular, even strides.
3. Swing your arms slightly with each stride, but use no other upper-body motion.

Compared with running, walking is less stressful to your knees, back, and all affected ligaments and joints. Even so, the increase in the popularity of the sport has resulted in an increase in minor complaints and injuries. Most are associated with pain or pressure along the outside borders of the foot. Other specific complaints include pain or irritation of the little toe, ankle sprain, pressure on the big toe, Achilles tendinitis, posterior tibial tendinitis (pain on the insides of the ankles), metatarsalgia (pain on the bottom of the feet behind the toes), irritated bunions, and plantar fasciitis (pain on the bottom of the heels). All of these problems can be addressed by your sports medicine physician, who will also be alert to the possibility that your walking shoe is the culprit. Generally speaking, anyone with a history of leg and foot injuries reduces the risk of such problems by walking.

The chief disadvantage of walking, as I've noted, is that a very fit person will find it difficult, if not impossible, to attain target heart range by walking, even by raising their pace. Younger people, in particular, may not be able to achieve target heart rate before reaching a biomechanical ceiling, finding themselves mechanically unable to walk faster without breaking into a job. (Most people reach this ceiling at approximately 5 miles per hour, or 12 minutes a mile.) The answer may be the specialized form of exercise known as race walking.

Race Walking

You might achieve your target heart range by race walking, a specially defined form of exercise that is becoming increasingly popular with the exercise elite. In fact, race walking is spreading so quickly among serious exercisers that there are race-walking marathons.

In this exercise, the upper body becomes more involved than in regular walking or running, because you swing the arms and shoulders. This exaggerated action promotes the toning capability of the exercise and provides added aerobic benefit. With the correct movement of legs and feet, your hips will swing naturally, giving you ease in performing this particular form of walking.

Because race walking uses both front and back muscles in the legs—as opposed to running, which overdevelops the front muscles and leaves the leg's back muscles relatively weak—this exercise will develop well-balanced leg muscles. Consequently, race walkers are less likely than runners to suffer from shin splints, Achilles tendinitis, and syndromes of overuse. Women, who typically gain weight between knees and waist, particularly appreciate race walking's tendency to trim off excess fat from hips, buttocks, thighs, and the backs of upper arms. Maryanne Torrellas, one of the top women race walkers in the United States, says she burns off more than 400 calories an hour when working out. Pace is still the key, however, to working up to your heart range.

You have to begin slowly, of course, and pay particular attention to your technique.

1. Never completely leave the ground, as in running. Your lead foot touches down before your rear foot is pulled up.
2. Do not bend your supporting leg at the knee when it passes under your body. Keep it straight.
3. Use smooth, gliding movements and walk tall. Use the rear leg for a good strong pushoff.
4. Keep arms always at a 90-degree angle and hands loosely clenched. Swing your arms from the shoulders so that they brush by your waistband and rise above your chest.
5. Land squarely on the heel, with your toes pointed slightly upward.
6. Do not try to exaggerate your hip movements. When one foot lands in front of the other in a straight line, your hips will move properly.

Race walking is a lot of fun, once you learn how, and dedicated race walkers are pleased to find that their stomachs and upper thighs are beautifully firmed up and toned. A mild warning: to learn the correct stride and to devise the program that's best for you, it's advisable to contact one of the many race-walking organizations around the country. (Addresses are listed with those of other exercise-oriented groups in Appendix C.)

On the down side, some people feel that the vigorous arm swinging, hip bobbing, and knee straining of high-intensity race walking make the sport less efficient in maintaining fitness than jogging at the same pace. On the other hand, at least one study has demonstrated that the racewalker's upper and lower body burn more fuel than the runner's at a similar speed. For example, at 5 miles per hours, the runner burned 480 calories, the racewalker 530. Not all experts are convinced. Certainly, very fit young people may find they quickly hit the biomechanical ceiling and have to begin running to achieve their target heart range. But race walkers who love their exercise remain interested and dedicated to it for a lifetime.

Consider this experience reported by Howard Jacobson, president of the New York Walkers Club, in his comprehensive guide, *Racewalk to Fitness:* "I was doing a fast 10 miles along the service road to the Long Island Expressway. At about 6 miles out, I got the strangest feeling. I felt like my head was detached from my body, like I was an 'observer of me.' I was very loose, very relaxed, moving very fast, and felt light-headed. Every once in a while since then, I go through it again. Always when I am alone. Always when I am fast and fluid. Who said walkers don't get high?" (In his book, by the way, Jacobson provides an extremely useful systematic twelve-week guide for beginning race walkers.)

George Sheehan, M.D., recommends race walking in *Doctor George Sheehan's Medical Advice for Runners* for athletes recuperating from injuries. "Race walking is the perfect sport for recuperants from some other sports," he writes. "The ailing athlete who turns to racewalking will find himself on the mend."

Running/Jogging

If burning off calories is important to your long-term goals, you'll be interested to know that a University of Missouri study has shown that jogging can use up to 35 more calories per hour than walking. At the same time, it also burns off a slightly higher percentage of fat.

One observation is indisputable: you are rarely going to see a heavy runner. "Most people are fat not from overeating but from lack of exercise," writes Dr. Mona Shangold, author of *The Complete Sports Medicine Book for Women*. On average, running burns energy at the rate of about 100 calories per mile, at the same time reducing fat deposits and building muscle. As a general rule, the more you weigh and the faster you run, the more calories you will lose.

You should not rely solely upon weight tables for estimating your caloric losses, however, because body weight could include a heavily muscular build. The key is body fat, which should be at an average level of 12 to 15 percent for men, 22 to 25 percent for women. Your physician can use calipers to measure skinfold and determine your percentage of body fat.

If you are larger framed or more muscular than the average, it is difficult to compare your performance as a runner with the running times of others in your age group. You can contact the Clydesdale Runners Association (see Appendix C), a group that has devised equivalent times for runners of various weights in the 10K and the marathon.

You will have to work your way up gradually to the kind of running program that is going to trim you down to the low body fat of marathoners, but you will have plenty of company along the way. Running, despite all of the media attention and Yuppie trendiness associated with it over the past few years, has not peaked in national popularity. Quite the opposite. If you decide to become a runner, you will have the added pleasure of meeting other enthusiasts almost everywhere you go. Running clubs, now established in cities and most smaller communities, not only offer companionship and camaraderie but also training workshops, workout tips, and, when you become more skilled, information about races for virtually every type and level of runner. If your sedentary friends or relatives don't get excited about your day's achievements in running, it's a safe bet that there's someone at work, at church, or in the neighborhood who is eager to share war stories about this extremely popular form of exercise. That is a terrific advantage, psychologically, when you're just starting to exercise.

Follow the advice of Maureen Custy-Roben, who won San Diego's Holiday Bowl Marathon in 1987: "Keep running fun to improve. Vary your workouts, run different routes, and run with friends to heighten the enjoyment. If you hate to run, you'll quit." For a really concentrated approach, you might consider one of the adult running camps that have sprung up around the country in recent years. Catering to beginners as well as to the initiated, they offer encouragement in the form of bucolic settings, new friends, coaching, lectures, social activities, and regenerated enthusiasm. (See Appendix C.)

In addition, running offers a fast-paced change of scenery and unrivaled flexibility: you can run almost anywhere, at almost any time, and you don't have to invest in or carry around a lot of equipment. One of my patients, a corporate pilot, runs wherever his job takes him: Paris, Singapore, Caracas, Beijing, Jidda, Algiers, Perth, Milan, Kuala Lampur. I do not exaggerate. This enviable change of scenery makes running "effortless," he says, and is the best way to get to know a new city right away. Most of us will have to be content with less exotic venues, but that's okay. Diversion is where you find it.

Nor is running likely to be hampered by weather, in the temperate zone. "The ideal exercise weather is forty to eighty-five degrees Fahrenheit with the humidity less than sixty percent and the wind velocity less than fifteen miles per hour," according to Dr. Kenneth Cooper. Outside those boundaries, adjustments in clothing, time of day, or length of exercise can make it possible to run safely and comfortably.

I can think of only two restrictions for you to remember. First, you should always wait two to three hours after eating before you run. Otherwise, you will be uncomfortable and unable to perform at peak. Second, always run at the same time of day, once you've settled upon a schedule. That kind of commitment will help ensure that you don't fall behind and will reaffirm for your, and for others, the seriousness of your program.

Like walking, running will strengthen the muscles in your lower back and legs but will have little or no effect upon your upper body and your quadriceps, the muscles in front of your thighs. At the same time, running does afford opportunities for contracting illness and injury. You should take the following four warnings to heart:

1. Don't overwork your body. The results can include continual fatigue, chronic soreness, and cold symptoms.
2. Don't let your muscles get overtightened because of not stretching adequately.
3. Be alert for a faulty foot strike, either because of incorrect running style or structural problems in your feet.
4. Make sure you're wearing the proper shoes.

In addition, runners must remember the importance of adequate rest, or not stubbornly trying to run when they have an illness, no matter how minor.

When you first feel any dull ache in a muscle, joint, tendon, or ligament, you should slow down for a few sessions or switch to another sport, like swimming, that does not strain the affected area. If the pain has not abated within a week, you should see your physician. Ignoring such pain is not brave or stoic; it's stupid and potentially dangerous.

Even champions forget this simple rule. Herb Lindsay, holder of the 10-mile American road record, did so in the 1984 Olympic trials 10,000. "In the heats, I blistered badly and didn't get them treated properly," he recalls. "The blisters came back in the final, and I wasn't able to put my fitness to the test. I just blew it by not getting proper treatment."

Marathon Injuries

For marathoners, injuries can be especially serious. To prevent injuries in long-distance and marathon running, my friend Dr. Andres Rodriguez has come up with ten medical commandments based upon his experiences as medical director of the New York City Marathon.

DR. ANDRES RODRIGUEZ'S
TEN MEDICAL COMMANDMENTS

1. Make sure that you are physically fit for the running activities that you are undertaking.
2. Train properly.
3. Follow guidelines for proper nutrition.
4. Maintain adequate hydration before, during, and after the race.
5. Perform warm-up and stretching exercises before, and cool-down and stretching exercises after the run.

6. Dress properly, according to the weather.
7. Use proper, comfortable shoes—*not* a new pair.
8. Watch the condition of the running surface or road.
9. Do not overdo it; run at your own pace.
10. Listen to your body: slow down, or even stop, if you do not feel well.

Training

There are two main approaches to developing your potential as a runner: you can either gradually increase the length of your runs, in terms of time or distance, or gradually increase your running speed.

If you decide to work on your *duration*, remember the 20 percent guide; never increase how far or how long you run by more than 20 percent of your weekly total. For example, if you generally run 30 minutes three times a week, or a total of 90 minutes, you would increase your time by no more than 18 minutes in one session, or up to 48 minutes. If you run 5 miles three times a week, or a weekly total of 15 miles, you would begin increasing your distance in one session by no more than 3 miles.

If you prefer to develop by gradually increasing your *speed*, you may want to try the popular method known as Long, Slow Distance (LSD). First, you build endurance by running farther than normal for you at a pace slower than you normally run. With a gentle, even stride, you run about one minute per mile slower than your usual pace. Second, after your endurance has increased, you begin raising your pace for the longer distance, but do not run all-out. Run faster, but about 15 to 30 seconds per mile slower than your average. This fast running should not total more than 20 percent of your entire week's running.

After you have developed your running skills, you may want to consider specializing in a particular event, concentrating on the particular challenges and rewards it offers. Julie

Brown, who won the World Cross-Country Championships in 1975 and is the second fastest American woman marathoner, offers a champion's perspective on specialization: "I always wanted the marathon to be my event, but I never trained properly for it. My problem was I ran every distance. I ran track, the roads, indoors, marathons. I never specialized. Even though I had a lot of good races, that held me back from having a great one."

Walking, Race Walking, Running on the Curve

If you have never exercised before and are not aerobically trained, you are not going to get on the Curve in six weeks, as experienced exercisers probably will. For the first week, you want to begin by walking briskly in every session, never pushing yourself to exhaustion or in any way straining. You may need to start as slowly as three 10-minute sessions per week. Do not push! If you feel like a little jog from time to time, do it, but don't overdo it. Practice taking your pulse, but don't aim for target heart rate at this point. Your aim in the beginning is to keep your mood level at level zero. If you go below that, you are exercising too much. Shorten your exercise periods until you return to mood level zero and then begin to lengthen them again.

Whether you're inexperienced or experienced, certain things are true for everyone in the first week. First, you must get into the habit of making your diary entries: length of session, pace of exercise, mood level afterward. Second, you must follow all of the advice I've given earlier about proper preparation and proper warming down, no matter how mildly you exercise in the beginning. If you feel soreness afterward, you are doing too much.

In the second week, beginning exercisers should increase

the amount of walking or jogging during each session, but not the length of the session. The point now is to develop a skill you can use safely and enjoyably for the rest of your life, not to become a competitive runner within a few weeks. Gradually, by two minutes per session, you can lengthen your exercise periods. The goal is to build up to 20-minute sessions, but if jogging ever becomes a strain during a workout, switch to walking until you are comfortable again.

Phase I ends for you, as for experienced exercisers, when you can exercise 20 minutes in your target heart range three times a week and maintain your mood at level zero or slightly above. For Phase II, all exercisers will have to decide upon a method of determining pace. You can record your workouts in terms of beats per minute or minutes per mile; whichever you choose, you will stick with that method in your diary so that you can fine-tune your performance in Phase III. Some of my patients like to use a pedometer, a simple, lightweight device that measures how far you walk or run. It can help you keep accurate records in your diary.

Many active people agree with the opinion of Melanie Roffers, a nutritional biochemist who is a director of San Francisco's Nob Hill Health Club: "Runners *are* sexier. To me, a beautiful, sexy body is one with good muscle definition. Not that everyone should look like a body builder, but to the extent that running helps eliminate men's pot bellies and women's flabby thighs, it makes them look sexier."

On that note, let's move on to a wide variety of sports that have broad appeal and are readily adaptable to Maharam's Curve. They do not include team sports, which obviously do not lend themselves to the pacing required. On the other hand, using other forms of exercise to get on the Curve can bring about remarkable improvements in your performance and attitude in team sports. From swimming to circuit training, rope jumping to stair climbing, the next chapter offers quite a variety. You may want to save yourself some time by turning to the Index and looking up the type of exercise that interests you, but I'd suggest you give each exercise at least a glance. You may find that a particular advantage—say, cardiovascular improvement combined with ease or inexpensiveness of access—will attract you to a previously unfamiliar activity that is just right for you at this time in your life.

CHAPTER THIRTEEN

SWIMMING, AEROBICS, CYCLING, AND MORE

> When I'm in the water, I couldn't be happier. I like swimming because I can't hear anything when I'm in the water. I'm completely at ease with myself as I move along and feel every muscle and fiber in my body working in sync. It can't be beat.
>
> —Skip Storch,
> after swimming the Hudson River 153 miles
> from Albany, New York, to Manhattan

Swimming

If you've read this far, my personal bias is no secret: for me, swimming is the most refreshing, relaxing, and stimulating of all sports. No form of exercise gives *me* more pleasure. (If you already feel that strongly about a specific sport or exercise, you need not read this chapter.) Not everyone shares my feeling, of course, but it is fair to say that swimming is the kind of exercise that is available to most people and can be easily alternated with other activities in order to achieve a well-balanced exercise program. About 30,000,000 Americans choose this sport for rehabilitative, exercise, and competitive aims every year.

Along with its relative convenience, swimming offers a surprising bonus to those who want to burn calories. Often, the swimmer uses more calories than the cyclist or even the runner. For one thing, you have to propel the body forward, fight water drag, and remain afloat—all at the same time. These aims require calorie-eating energy. In addition, most swimming strokes involve the use of upper body, arms, and legs—a further drain upon energy. "A half-hour in the pool is like a fifteen-mile run for me," says Joan Benoit Samuelson, who won the gold medal in the 1984 Olympic Marathon.

Even as an active swimmer burns more calories, his or her heart rate does not increase as much as that of exercisers on land because of the cooling effects of water. Generally speaking, your heart rate per minute in your target heart range *while exercising* will be about 15 beats per minute slower when swimming than when running or aerobic dancing. Therefore, swimmers have to make a slight adjustment in the formula for determining their target heart range. Subtract your age from 205 (not the standard 220) before multiplying by the usual 65 to 85 percent.

Puzzling news for the weight-conscious swimmer was widely published in the late 1980s. Several studies seemed to indicate that swimmers did not necessarily lose weight or, even worse, might even gain weight as they exercised.

Don't panic. As is often the case, these studies were misinterpreted or oversimplified in the popular press. For example, Dr. Graham Gwinup ran a complex study at the University of California, Irvine, that involved 45 overweight women. They were asked to increase their exercise time suddenly to 60 minutes a day and engage in either walking, cycling, or swimming. Over the six-month duration of this study, cyclers and walkers lost weight, but swimmers steadily got heavier. Probably the weight gain came from added muscle while the swimmers' body fat stayed the same. On the other hand, because the relaxing, soothing climate of swimming can lull the exerciser, it can become easy to fall into the trap of gliding along, completely missing your target heart range. The researchers involved in the Irvine study and other similar projects have agreed that maintaining target heart range throughout a swimming routine will burn calories and produce weight loss. An additional factor is that cold water prompts the swimmer's body to produce more insulation in the form of fat. The temperature of the water also prevents the body's metabolic rate from rising rapidly and stimulating your appetite mechanism. To increase loss of calories, therefore, you have to swim at a fast pace. If you swim at a leisurely pace, humming an Irish dirge, you will only burn 50 calories more in 20 laps than you would just by floating like a log.

Experienced exercisers may be surprised to learn that a recent study proved that both run training and swim training, when performed near absolute intensity, achieved essentially the same significant increase in treadmill VO_2 max. The 37 males in the study, which took place at the University of California, Davis, were all considered sedentary. For a period of 11 ½ weeks, some were run-trained, others were swim-trained, and the rest were controls. The runners and swimmers, who trained three days a week, increased 28 and 25 percent, respectively, in treadmill VO_2 max. In other words, the study suggests that running and swimming are equally effective in increasing cardiorespiratory fitness.

In swimming as in all other forms of exercise, it is not only *what* you do but *how* you do it. That applies to proper form as well as level of exertion. Videotapes, sports events on TV, books, and local coaches are good sources of help when you are starting out or when you have become lazy about your swimming style. Bad habits are easy to pick up, hard to break.

The physical advantages of swimming, as opposed to running, aerobics, and other weight-bearing exercise, include a decreased likelihood of joint and other musculoskeletal injuries. Runners who have developed back problems often find that they can swim without aggravation. To take an extreme example, Dave Horning, a triathlete from San Francisco, took up swimming after he broke his back in a skiing accident. Another advantage is that swimming can increase bone density to an extent—even if not so much as weight-bearing exercises like walking and running.

Because swimming provides a challenge to almost all of your muscles, you may find that your arms and upper back need to be trained, even if your heart and lungs are fit from other types of exercise.

In the beginning, you need to start slowly and build up to a steady pace gradually. For muscle balance and injury prevention, you should vary your strokes. To avoid misaligning the bones of the neck, alternate breathing between the right and left side of the body. Alleviate the strain on your neck by looking down rather than ahead as you swim. To avoid the possibility of jamming the spine's rear joints, keep your pelvis down and your back flat. Don't be fooled by the soothing waters: you can overdo it, so be alert for any dizziness, chest pain, difficulty in breathing, or pain in the muscles and joints.

If boredom threatens to set in, you should try the popular routine known as *pyramids*. The image is apt: in one session, you gradually increase the length of your swims to a peak, then gradually decrease them. For example, you might swim 100 yards, rest five seconds, swim 200 yards, rest five seconds, and so on until you reach your goal for the day. At that point, you go into reverse, as it were, dropping 100 yards from each swim, resting five seconds in between, and ending with your initial length of 100 yards.

One practical disadvantage of swimming, of course, may be the problem of finding year-round access to a pool. The physical disadvantages of swimming are few, however, though certainly worth looking out for. Most stem from lack of proper warm-up or technique. Any swimmer should pay special attention to my discussion of stretching, beginning on page 76, and should study the stroke he or she wants to pursue. You can get advice from a sports medicine physician or from someone who specializes in swimming: a competitive swimmer, a team coach at your local high school or college, or a Red Cross water-safety instructor.

Who knows? You may become as addicted to swimming as people like me, or English Channel swimmer Charlie "The Tuna" Chapman. "Man against water is the ultimate marathon," he says. "I'm thinking about going the distance, but I'm enjoying myself, too. Swimming is the most relaxing thing I know."

Swimming on the Curve

It takes ingenuity to get on the Curve with a program confined to swimming. You have to start slowly and work up gradually, paying attention to the special difficulties of determining your target heart rate, and resisting the constant temptation to relax and glide through the water.

Phase I will end when you've developed a comfortable stroke that keeps you in your (revised) target heart range for 20-minute sessions three times a week.

In Phase II, you will home in on your pace. One way of keeping a diary is to count the number of laps per 20-minute session. (Obviously, the length of the pool is a factor in this reckoning.) Another method is to buy one of the waterproof belts available from trendy sports outlets and specialty catalogs. They are designed for carrying a water-resistant Walkman at the back of your waist as you swim, pacing yourself to the music you choose until you find the optimum beats per minute.

Water aerobics may fool you. Exactly what it sounds like— aerobics in the water—this form of exercise is slower and more controlled than similar exercise on dry land, but the results can be very similar. The slower movements of aqua-aerobics, however, will require slower music, a range between 124 and 136 beats per minute (as opposed to the typical range of 136 to 160 beats per minute for land aerobics). Movements should involve the whole body, back and forth, side to side, and the surface of the water should not "boil" because of your efforts. Despite the gentler look and feel, water aerobics can burn off an average of 400 calories per hour, including 77 percent of body fat. Land-based aerobics gets rid of only 42 percent of fat in an hour of exercise.

Many injured athletes find that regular exercise in the water helps them regain strength without putting strain and pressure on tender joints and muscles. Water's buoyancy also reduces pressure on the spine and lower back. Running in the water, for example, takes advantage of the soothing effect of the water—and the absence of the pull of gravity—to heal a muscle pull, or a tendon or ligament injury. It also can give you a great cardiovascular workout, but you have to start slowly: tread the water for 2 to 3 minutes, then begin running. You're likely to get discouraged at first, if you aren't prepared to rest frequently, but patience will get you up to the 20-minute workouts three times a week you can use for the Curve.

Water aerobics have been especially attractive to my women patients who want to exercise but protest that "I don't like to perspire." In the cool water of the pool, you won't perspire noticeably. You actually do to some extent, of course, so anyone doing water aerobics or swimming must remember to drink water to rehydrate.

As with any other aerobics class, you should check out the background of your instructor, who ideally should have training in water safety as well as in exercise. "Aqua-aerobics is not just land aerobics done in a pool," warns Carol Kennedy, the fitness director at the University of Illinois. "The teacher should have water-safety training as well as an exercise background."

To begin, you could try three of the most popular aquatic exercises:

1. Aqua jacks: Go to shoulder-depth water and extend
   your arms, palms down, just below the surface. Jump
   upward, simultaneously crossing your arms in front of
   you horizontally and crossing your legs at the ankles.
2. Aqua cycling: As you float on your stomach or back,
   grasp the side of the pool and bring one knee after the
   other up to your chest, as if you were actually cycling
   underwater.
3. Pumping water: Move to chest-high water and jog in
   place, all the while punching the water vigorously with
   your fists closed underwater.

Water Aerobics on the Curve

Don't be fooled by the coolness of the water, the fine sun-
shine, or the smoothness of your movements: water aerobics
can be exhausting, and you do not want to overtax yourself.
Listen to your body. Perhaps as little as 10 minutes three
times a week is enough in the beginning. Take your pulse
during exercises that allow you to pause briefly with your
wrist out of the water, but don't go immediately for your
target rate. For the first few sessions, your goal is to reach
mood level zero and maintain it. If you have trouble, look
back at the beginning of Chapter Eight to make sure you
understand my explanation of this first phase of the Curve.

After the first week of becoming familiar with the different
exercises and concentrating on the ones that work best for
you or give you the most pleasure, you can begin exercising
more strenuously, but not yet for a longer period. Only in
the third week or—even later, depending on how you feel—
should you begin to increase the length of your exercise sessions, perhaps by as little as 2 extra minutes per week.

Phase I ends when you have built up to exercising for
three 20-minute sessions per week in your target heart range,
without straining or overtiring yourself. (By this point, you

will certainly know what I mean about the deceptively easy look of water aerobics.) If everything is going well, your mood level will maintain at zero, or even slightly above.

For the special pleasures of Phase II, you will have to pay careful attention to your exercise pace, remembering to record each workout in your diary, to keep checking your heart rate as necessary, and to keep your eyes on the mood cards. It may help to use the water-resistant Walkmans that some swimmers depend upon for pacing. Or your pool, like many, may have a large clock on the wall with a second hand. Whatever method you choose for keeping track of your all-important individual pace, you must stick with it into Phase III, where fine-tuning can begin.

Aerobic Dance—Any Style

The combination of exercise and music, as Jane Fonda was the first to show the nation, is probably the most successful way of getting nonexercisers on their feet and working out. Her calisthenics-to-music approach was limited, but it did open up a broad new world of dance exercising.

Your favorite song, as I've suggested earlier, can be a stronger motivator and reinforcement to exercise than any pep talk I can offer on these pages. The beat and rhythm not only provide a back beat to keep your body moving and in sync; they also act as a useful distraction, keeping you from thinking about muscles that might begin to ache or wondering when your second wind is going to kick in. Instead, you join your senses with the music, knowing that you can hold on until the song ends. If you've ever participated in an aerobics class, you know what I mean. The more established and sophisticated the particular program, the more likely that the dance tapes have been designed specifically to bring you from warm-up through low-impact aerobic dance to high-intensity exercise, with individual songs keyed to certain stretches, areas of body development, mood altering, and warming down.

Don't be suspicious of the benefits of classes that specialize in low-impact aerobics—routines that require that one foot be on the floor at all times. Such low-impact routines have been created to avoid the high injury rates associated with high-impact aerobics, which incorporate a lot of jumping movements. Low-impact routines will get you up to 75 to 95 percent of your maximum heart rate if performed with high intensity. The class instructor will know how to help you increase your intensity gradually until you are using an effectively fast pace, large steps, and vigorous arm movements.

Aerobics classes are likely to be readily available where you live. Most health clubs and Y's offer a varied, convenient schedule of aerobic dance. The possibilities seem endless. The latest variation in New York is the "world-beat" class, aerobics performed to the beat of live drummers using the intricate rhythms of African, Latin, Haitian, and Brazilian music. "We're into fun, not gain from pain," says the instructor in a world-beat class called Reggaecize. And in some areas of the country, you can exercise to a TV program called "Working Out for Jesus with Beverly." This instructor uses rap songs based upon Biblical texts.

Such an abundance requires some sensible caution, however. You will want to check into the credentials of the teacher of any class that interests you. I'm not suggesting that a medical degree should be a requirement, but the instructor who takes responsibility for your dance exercise should have education in exercise physiology as well as some dance training. Good looks, good intentions, and an engaging smile are not enough. Don't be shy about asking. Any legitimate sponsoring organization will be happy to provide this background information.

The ultimate convenience, as the ads suggest, is indeed the privacy of your own VCR. Since the groundbreaking Fonda video, and its spectacular commercial success, the actress herself has produced much more sophisticated, effective tapes, and the market offers a panoply of competing exercise videos, many geared to highly specialized audiences. Rent a few until you find the one that makes the most sense for your needs. I think that buying at least one is a good idea, because you can key your pacing and your psychological reactions to a routine that becomes familiar.

Be warned that, no matter how much fun they are, all of the variations of aerobic dance—jump rope, tap dance, water aerobics—still require serious concentration, correct technique, and proper preparation. Approach them just as runners approach their exercise period. Be just as careful as swimmers in figuring out your target heart range and appropriate pacing. The use of a metronome, for example, is especially effective in pacing your dance exercise. One song can be used to set the base pace on the metronome; as you speed up or slow down in plotting your curve during Phase III, the metronome will help you decide which other song can be a better guide to achieving your maximum exercise high. Usually, you will find yourself working out to music in the range of 136 to 160 beats per minute.

Traditional dance forms can be even more fulfilling than aerobic dancing, which is basically a combination of a few rudimentary dance steps with a slew of calisthenics.

Tap dance, for example, is one of the greatest of aerobic exercises. You utilize both your upper and lower body while keeping your own beat with your tapping feet. No, it's not as easy as Gregory Hines makes it look, but some people get hooked in their first lesson. And weekly lessons are definitely necessary. This is a very special skill, but it can be learned gradually under a graded method of instruction. According to Dr. Robert Baird, amateur tap dancer, New York City internist, and assistant professor of medicine at New York Medical College, "Tap dancing is one of the great exercises . . . especially good for your peripheral vascular circulation." The point is to have fun while you exercise, not take your act on the road. And perhaps you have the gift. . . .

Serious *ballet* requires much more in the way of technique, strength, flexibility, and regular practice, but it can be an excellent toning tool even at the beginner level. We've all seen the Sunday magazine feature stories and TV clips about ballet classes for football teams or hockey jocks, and you can certainly sharpen your exercise skills and timing in ballet. Aerobically, however, it will not provide enough target range exercise to be used as your primary exercise routine, unless you are working at the Baryshnikov level.

Even *ballroom dancing*, believe it or not, can be effective exercise, if you are doing Latin American or modern dance sequences rather than a shuffling two-step. A study Down Under showed that ballroom dancers can get more than 80 percent of maximum oxygen consumption.

Dancing on the Curve

If you have never aerobic danced before, or have been away from the floor for some time, you should start with 10-minute sessions, concentrating on learning the steps and flowing with the music. Build your way up to 20-minute sessions that maintain your target heart range, without taking rests between each number. Just keep bouncing up and down until the next song starts.

You move from Phase I into Phase II by finding the beats-per-minute rhythm that works best for you. As you rise on your Curve, enjoying the sensations of Phase II, you might divert yourself by planning ahead for Phase III. Buy the commercial tapes and decide which songs you like, or experiment with a metronome and music that you already have around the house. You'll want to choose songs faster than your pace song in Phase II, but give yourself a range so that you can move back and forth incrementally as you fine-tune your pacing in Phase III.

This general advice applies to all types of dance—aerobic dance, tap, ballroom, ballet, salsa, or even the minuet, if you really work at it. In each instance, your goal is to find the music that gives you the beat to work toward 80 percent of your heart capacity. If you like rock or pop music, cable TV offers the added interest of visuals on the music channels, but you might not always find a sequence of videos that is close enough to the pace you need. Perhaps you can purchase a rock or dance video, however, that gives you the right pace. Anything that helps keep you diverted while you work toward your exercise goals is a valuable tool for increasing your fitness.

Stepping

Inexpensive, convenient, taking up very little space, the hottest new exercise is known as "step aerobics" or "bench-stepping." Stepping allows you to work out so strenuously that you can reach 90 percent of your maximum heart rate while burning a lot of calories: 10 calories per minute if you take 20 steps per minute, 16 calories per minute if you take 30 steps per minute.

At the same time, step aerobics is adaptable to almost all levels of fitness, offers minimal stress to the musculoskeletal system, and requires only low-impact force. It strengthens the lower body while improving cardiovascular fitness. In fact, many older readers will be familiar with stepping from the doctor's office, where the step-test was once used to assess cardiovascular fitness. Step aerobics is now recommended often for rehabilitation and strengthening of injured knees and ankles.

Bench-stepping is just what it sounds like: you step up and down at a regular pace on a small bench or box, alternating feet. Stepping requires proper attention to form and a bench that is the right height for you. If you are an intermediate to advanced exerciser of average height, the bench should be 6 to 8 inches high. Six inches is the maximum for the beginning exerciser, people shorter than average, and anyone prone to knee injury.

If your bench is the proper height, you should be able to make a 90-degree angle with your upper and lower leg as you step up. Every 4 to 6 seconds, glance down at the bench in order to stay aware of its height and location. Good posture is essential as you work out, so stay aware constantly of body alignment.

To begin your workout, place the heel of one foot (the lead foot) firmly in the center of the box or bench, step up, and bring the other foot firmly alongside the lead foot to stand on the bench with both feet, then step down to the floor with the lead foot and bring the other foot alongside. At the end of each minute, you should switch the foot you are using as the lead.

As you exercise, never bend your knees more than 90 degrees. Never pivot on a bent, supporting knee. At all times, remember to stay aware of how stable you feel as well as the amount of pressure on your knees. As with any other form of exercise, remember the importance of warming up, stretching, and warming down.

TIPS FOR PREVENTING INJURY

1. Have your physician or a sports medicine specialist give you a postural and flexibility evaluation to find out whether or not you are prone to developing knee problems.
2. Be alert for the early signs and symptoms of knee problems: a cracking or clicking noise when you walk, stiffness or pain after sitting for long periods, trouble getting out of a chair, or pain when you walk up stairs.
3. Always remember to increase the intensity of your bench workouts gradually.

Throughout this exercise, you should not experience strain in your legs or buttocks, pain in the knee area, or excessive fatigue. If you do, the bench is probably too high. Step aerobics is designed to tax one muscle most of all: the heart.

Stepping on the Curve

Don't rush. This is another exercise that looks deceptively easy, but you can push too hard, too fast, and cause yourself some nagging problems. Slow and steady is the motto to remember. In your early sessions, exercise only to the verge of discomfort, not until you drop. Probably, the new exerciser will want to start with 10-minute sessions, getting used to the challenge of a new routine and the new feelings in an untrained body. Experienced exercisers may be able to start with 20-minute sessions but may also want to pay special attention to fighting off boredom with music or television. If boredom with this repetitious exercise encourages you to speed up your pace too quickly, it may not be the right exercise for you.

Both new and experienced exercisers should aim during Phase I for consistency at mood level zero. Too much exercise too soon will send you below that level. When that happens, pull back and increase the length of your workouts only gradually, perhaps by only 2 minutes per session. The goal for all exercisers is to be in your target heart range throughout three 20-minute sessions per week. Making entries in your exercise diary should become a part of your routine. Learning how to take your pulse at regular intervals without letting your heart rate slide is also important. And remember to review and follow closely the rules of preparation for exercise. Stepping can be as hard on the body, if you do not prepare and do not warm down, as exercises that may seem more complicated or demanding.

Once you've attained your goal—three weekly sessions 20

minutes long each in target heart range—you are in Phase II. This is a time for relaxing and enjoying the changes in your body and the continued elevation of your mood. The word "relax," however, does not apply to record-keeping and pulse-taking. In Phase II, you have to pay close attention to finding and maintaining your individual pace. In Phase III, knowing that pace makes the difference between working up to the exercise high and regressing by falling off the Curve.

Rowing

Not the most conveniently accessible of sports, rowing has the attraction of demanding a great deal of exertion from the large muscle groups in each motion. Few forms of exercise burn calories as quickly. In fact, a recent study comparing the efforts of subjects on rowing machines with those on stationary bikes showed that the rowers burned many more calories than the cyclists.

Fortunately, the art and benefit of rowing can be almost as rewarding on the home exercise machine as on the winding Cam or Charles. Ronnie Barnes, head athletic trainer of the New York Giants football team, says that he gets his best workouts on his rower at home. You don't have to invest in the equipment yourself; most health clubs have some type of rowing machine on the premises, probably equipped with a calibrated mechanism that shows how fast you're going, how many calories you're burning, and, in some cases, what your heart range is at any given moment. This information can help you keep your eye on the prize as you exercise. The machine keeps a record, and you can concentrate on the enjoyment of working out and reaching for the exercise high. The calibrations can also help you set a goal. While you're waiting for your second wind, say, you can decide to keep going, no matter what, until you reach the 300-calorie mark. If the wind hasn't gusted at that point, you can set a higher mark and keep rowing. Remember, too, that rowing *is* rhythm. Steady pacing leads to the rewards of the high.

Rowing on the Curve

For pacing yourself in rowing, whether in the water or on an exercise machine, you will be using music with a fairly slow beat. If canoeing, you can work at a facer pace, of course.

As in all exercises, the beginning exerciser should be patient, working up gradually from 10-minute rowing sessions to longer ones. For the first week, the new exerciser should not try to reach target heart range; there is too much else to learn: how to take your pulse frequently and accurately, how to find a pace that you can maintain steadily without unnecessary strain or undue effort, how to let your body tell you when to slow down or speed up, and when to stop. Experienced exercisers may want to begin with longer sessions and work toward target heart range right away, but "experience" here implies a sensible understanding of how far to go in any one session.

By the second week, beginners should try to reach target heart range. From then on, perhaps by only 2 minutes per week, they should build up to sessions 20 minutes long, in target heart range, three times a week. New or experienced, all exercisers move into Phase II at that point.

Remember that you should enjoy yourself royally in Phase II. The joys of feeling more fit, better rested, happier, and sexier will delight you; at the same time, you should be working on your exercise diary, doing the cards regularly, and checking your pace at each session. Should you try music with a faster beat? Are you pushing too hard? This is the time for experimenting with pace, as dictated by changes in your mood. If you're exercising too vigorously or not vigorously enough, your mood levels will drop.

What you learn about pacing is essential, as I hope I've made clear in Chapter Ten, for the fine-tuning that is the essence of Phase III. You will be reaching for the exercise high, perhaps hoping for the rare experience of the "exercise explosion," but you will be focusing primarily on maintaining yourself on your individual Curve.

Cycling

Greg LeMond stirred us all when he became the first American to win the most prestigious of all bicycle races, the Tour de France. When he came back from injury and certain defeat to win again, he became an international hero. It is not surprising that his spectacular efforts have inspired a tremendous upsurge in cycling in the United States, even though most of us do not plan to meet the challenges of the Tour, a three-week, 3,000-mile competition that includes mountain climbs and 60-mile-per-hour descents.

Grueling as the Tour de France is, the TV and newspaper shots of coveys of cyclists racing through the Pyrenees or beside meadows conveyed the aesthetic appeal of the sport: you have the freedom to range throughout the countryside, finding continuing diversion as you maintain or fine-tune your exercise pace.

Once you establish your aerobic and endurance base, you are ready to work on maximizing the benefits of cycling by getting a multispeed bike. Find a bicycle salesman who is knowledgeable and willing to help you find the right fit. The wrong bike can be as physically dangerous as the wrong exercise shoe in other sports. If, for example, you know that you prefer cycling in the upright position, make sure you get upright handlebars instead of drop bars.

Take along this quick checklist devised by Marvin Bloom, M.D., an orthopedist and member of the editorial board of the American Running and Fitness Association.

DR. BLOOM'S BICYCLE-BUYING TIPS

1. Stand on the ground in your cycling shoes and straddle a prospective bike to check *frame size*. When you lift the bike by the handlebars so that the top tube touches your crotch, the tires should be 1 ½ to 2 inches off the ground. Today, by the way, all women's touring bikes have bars, just as men's bikes do. If you are a woman who chooses to use one of the old-fashioned bikes without a top tube, just imagine where the bar might ride.

2. *Saddle height* is correct if your knee is only slightly bent when you sit on the seat with your heel on a pedal that is at its lowest point.

3. *Saddle angle* is correct if the saddle and top of the bike frame are parallel to the ground, when viewed from the side.

4. *Handlebar height*: the top of the handlebars (drop-handlebar style) should be about 2 ½ inches below the top of the saddle.

5. For proper *handlebar tilt*, the bottom or dropped part of the handlebars should be parallel with the ground, or tilted down not more than 10 degrees.

6. The ball of your *foot* should rest on the center of the pedals.

7. Your *knee* should be directly over the pedal when the pedal is forward with the crank horizontal to the ground.

8. *Saddle-to-handlebar length*: The distance from the front of the saddle to the handelbar crossbar should be about the same as the distance from your elbow to your fingertips. Changing your handlebar extension will adjust this distance.

Begin slowly, working out only two to three days a week at first. From the start, take advantage of the particular virtue of cycling: vary the location of your rides, mixing hills with level surfaces in order to diversify the challenge and maximize aerobic capacity.

In addition to the standard warm-up and stretching regimen I've outlined previously, the cyclist should also loosen and warm the muscles further by pedaling slowly at the beginning of a workout and pulling back as the pedal passes the bottom of your stroke. LeMond suggests imagining that you're scraping mud off your shoe. For the first leg of your ride, you should maintain a smooth pace, saving the higher gears and maximum energy for journey's end. You don't want to be halfway around the reservoir or at the turning point of a strenuous round trip when you burn out! As the terrain changes, maintain a steady pedal rate by changing gears, shifting to a lower gear when you go up a hill. Use a lower range of gears if your knee is sore.

As with running, you train in cycling in terms of time, not mileage, always keeping close watch on your target heart range. On extended rides, you should carry plenty of water to prevent dehydration, as well as high-carbohydrate snacks. Cyclists in the Tour de France carry along a glucose polymer drink because it's easier to drink than eat in the intense competition. Cyclists should also be especially wary of the possibility of cramping. An ounce of prevention: eat and drink lightly and steadily.

If your daydreams veer toward the erotic while you're cycling, you are definitely not alone. In a poll of 1,675 cyclists tallied by *Bicycling* magazine in 1989, 84 percent reported that they think about sex while cycling, and two out of three claimed that they had become better lovers because of cycling. (On the other hand, people who race are less likely to daydream about sex than about cycling.)

As with rowing, today's increasingly ingenious and responsive machines can provide the benefits of cycling at your health club, though lacking the associated charms of potholes and exhaust fumes. A gauge will usually track your pace and expenditure of energy, and most machines provide a simulated landscape that provides schematized peaks and valleys to divert your imagination. . . . You become Le-Mond! Or perhaps you would rather become Miss America. Debbye Turner, winner of the title in 1989, added a daily indoor bike ride of 30 to 45 minutes to her exercise schedule in the last six months before the contest. Music and TV can help you prevent terminal boredom. One inventive health club in Oregon came up with the idea of giving French and Spanish lessons while a class of stationary cyclers pedaled away. They were a great success.

The machine, however, can't do everything for you; it is always essential to keep monitoring your exercise pace and your heart rate. If your health club offers a variety of stationary bicycles and ergometers, ask one of the trainers for advice in choosing the best for your needs and capabilities. If you decide to buy a machine, put your antennae up: read consumer magazines, get professional advice, talk to other exercisers. It's not my business to keep you from spending money foolishly on silly gadgets, but I urge you to buy the machine that actually helps you in attaining aerobic capacity and reaching your high on the Curve.

Cycling, if you watch where you're going, is not associated with any particular type of injuries. If you are prone to knee problems, though, be sure to keep the seat high enough to give your leg full extension when the pedal is all the way down. In this way, you eliminate undue wear and tear on the back of the knee cap. Change the position of your hands from time to time in order to avoid numbness, especially in your ring finger and little finger. Be alert for any persistent pain or numbness. You may have to change your riding position or adjust your seat's angle or height.

If you experience stiffness and soreness in your knees, even though your seat height is correct, the most likely explanation is that you are overdoing it. Perhaps you are not gradually increasing your workouts. To help prevent knee pain in the future, you should exercise specifically to de-

crease stress on your knees by strengthening your leg muscles. Try the following three exercises:

1. For quadriceps (the front of your thighs): Do leg lifts.
   Lying flat on your back, lift your leg slowly to 30 degrees, keeping the knee straight. Hold for a couple of
   seconds, then slowly lower the leg. Do three sets of 10
   to 12 repetitions with each leg. When that's easy, add
   ankle weights, working up gradually from 2 pounds to
   15 pounds.
2. For hamstrings (the back of your thighs): Do hamstring
   curls. Standing up and holding onto a support, keep
   your upper leg still and curl your lower leg backward
   until you've bent your knee 90 degrees. Hold it there
   for a couple of seconds, then slowly lower your leg. As
   with leg lifts, do three sets of 10 to 12 repetitions with
   each leg. If this exercise is easy, you may want to add
   ankle weights, gradually working up to 10 pounds.
3. For calves: Do toe raises. Standing with a barbell held
   on your shoulders behind your neck, do the same sets
   and repetitions as in the previous two exercises. Begin
   with about 20 pounds of weight and work up gradually,
   never adding more weight than feels comfortable and
   safe.

One serious warning: when you are cycling, you are a fool
not to wear an approved helmet. Most of the 1,300 deaths in
cycling accidents in the United States each year result from
head injuries. The record clearly shows that helmets reduce
the risk of brain injury by 88 percent, of head injury by 85
percent.

Cycling on the Curve

If you choose to get on the Curve by cycling, pay special
attention to all of the warnings above, especially to the pre-

vention of injuries. You can't go from sedentary life to 50-mile bike rides without risking serious trouble. Easy does it. In fact, new exercisers should not even try for target heart range or long trips during the first week of cycling, whether on country roads or in the gym. A 10-minute ride should be enough. Concentrate on learning to take your pulse; let your body decide which pace you should try in the beginning; pay attention to any protests that arise from any part of your body.

Experienced cyclists, of course, can begin high-intensity 20-minute-long workouts right away, but it is important not to let experience with cycling make you think that you can easily handle the new information you need for Maharam's Curve. In other words, you will have to pay just as much attention as new exercisers to your exercise diary and to doing the mood cards. As you do, your mood should be consistently at level zero.

For everyone, the transition from Phase I into Phase II occurs when you are cycling in target heart range for three 20-minute sessions each week. You have plenty of time during this phase to smell the roses; indeed, that is the point. Enjoy your exercise sessions and take note of all of the physical and mental improvements that exercising on the Curve has brought to your daily life. This is the time when many of my patients are so exhilarated that they get their spouses or friends to join them in the adventure of Maharam's Curve. At the same time, however, you are still doing the necessary work of determining your pace. Be sure that the song or strokes-per-minute or minute-miles standard you use is right for you. If your mood begins to fall, you are either working out too slowly or too quickly.

In Phase III, the knowledge you've acquired about individual pace will help you fine-tune your work on the Curve. As you cycle toward the top of a hill one sunlit afternoon, you might experience the "exercise explosion." Certainly, your fine-tuning will keep you at optimum mood levels, whether you are on a bicycle or an exercise machine.

Rope Jumping

No longer dismissed as a kid's game, rope jumping has been taken up by many adult exercisers as the exercise of the 1990s because of its many aerobic and fitness advantages. According to one researcher, one half-hour of continuous jumping is aerobically equivalent to one half-hour of running an 8 ½-minute mile. In addition, the jumper burns 360 calories in that strenuous half-hour. Rope jumping also improves endurance, overall coordination, timing, and rhythm, while strengthening upper and lower body muscles.

In practical terms, you need a space equivalent to a nine-foot cube with a stable but resilient floor, a durable but unweighted rope, and patience. Starting off too quickly will cool the ardor of any beginner, because rope jumping is extremely strenuous, burning up 9 to 12 times the energy you use when at rest. No matter how fit you are, you will want to begin by jumping at intervals, alternating brief spurts with such other activities as race walking, stationary cycling, or marching in place while you swing the rope like the arms of a windmill at your side. One expert advises that everyone begin rope jumping by repeating the following cycle four times: 1 minute of jumping, 2 minutes of an alternate activity. This total of 12 minutes can be lengthened gradually, with the total amount of jumping time rising about 2 minutes per week.

It would be best to check with a trainer or other expert so that your technique will afford minimal stress to calves and shins. You need shoes that give adequate cushioning to the forefoot and provide lateral stability. You use only your wrists and forearms to power the rope; your arms should be relaxed at the side of your body, elbows tucked to the waist. You begin with the "hop landing," both feet together, at a pace that is comfortable—probably 120 to 140 revolutions per minute. Music with a beat in that range will help you keep pace and coordinate the turning of the rope. Despite the common misconception that jumping puts undue stress on your knees, you are actually protecting the knee, dissipating energy over your entire foot and absorbing shock by landing on the ball of your foot. Your jump should be less than one inch, just enough to clear the rope on each swing. You can begin trying different footwork when you are adept with the hop landing.

For beginners, it makes sense to follow a gradual schedule like the following. The minutes for each session are the total minutes of actual jumping with the rope, not including any nonjumping movements:

Week 1	4 minutes	3 times weekly
Week 2	6 minutes	3 times weekly
Week 3	8 minutes	3 to 4 times weekly
Week 4	10 minutes	3 to 4 times weekly
Week 5	12 minutes	3 to 4 times weekly
Week 6	15 minutes	3 to 4 times weekly

Rope Jumping on the Curve

If you follow the advice above, particularly remembering to start off gradually if you have not been exercising regularly, rope jumping will get you on the Curve with a minimum of difficulty. The number of jumps per minute is a simple way of pacing yourself. Practice taking your pulse: you can let the rope dangle briefly, but still keep jumping slightly to help maintain your heart rate. Get into the habit of making notations in your exercise diary and doing the mood cards as part of your daily routine.

In the beginning, new exercisers should be careful not to push too hard. Start with fairly short workouts, perhaps only 10 minutes (or even less, if you are completely new to the exercise) three times a week, and do not attempt to achieve target heart range for the first week. Gradually increase the length of your sessions by 2 minutes or so each week, working out in your target heart range. Your aim is to reach mood level zero and sustain it. New and experienced exercisers alike will move into Phase II when they are comfortably doing three 20-minute workouts at target heart range each week.

In Phase II, rope jumping should give you great pleasure in each session. It helps if you can find music that has the same beat as the pace that works best for you at this point. If your mood levels should drop, your pace is either too fast or too slow for your present level of fitness. Adjust it and change the music you use, until you are feeling physically and emotionally happy again.

In Phase III, you will be fine-tuning, and that will require close attention to your pace. The goal here is to reach optimum mood level and sustain it. Finding that perfect balance may require experimentation, but there's no reason to worry about that. Take your time. Don't neglect your exercise diary. When you make changes in your exercise pace, don't go too far in one direction or the other, and give yourself at least three sessions for assessing the effects of the new pace. As you experiment, you might reach the "exercise explosion." Definitely you will be able to manipulate the link between exercise and mood that is the revolutionary idea behind Maharam's Curve.

Cross-Country Skiing; Speed, Ice, and Roller Skating

You have heard all your life that cross-country skiing is the perfect all-around sport. That's right. It is. You get an incredible aerobic workout. You get equal toning for the muscle groups in your upper and lower body. It works all of the body's major muscles and burns up more calories than any other form of exercise. (Recently, researchers discovered that exercisers using a NordicTrack cross-country-ski exercise machine used up more than 1,000 calories an hour.) Outdoors in the winter air or indoors on the simulating machines, this rhythmic sport is an especially efficient pathway to Maharam's Curve.

For those proficient in both activities, a mile of cross-country skiing is roughly equivalent to running the same distance. Runners cannot immediately switch to cross-country skiing, however, because, as in swimming, the upper body must be trained or soreness will result. Perhaps surprisingly, many people whose arthritis makes walking or running painful can enjoy cross-country skiing, which is less stressful on the joints.

Whether on the trail or in the gym, be sure to get expert instruction or you run the risk of exercising improperly. If you're used to downhill skiing, you might not immediately adjust to the subtly different challenges and rewards of this sport. Some people think that it's more like snowshoeing than downhill skiing, because you are emphasizing the constant rhythmic pace. (Downhill skiing, even if you are in the high altitudes of Vail or Davos, or terrifying yourself by attempting Tuckerman's Ravine, does not provide the aerobics necessary for getting on the Curve.)

The indoor version of cross-country skiing, most popularly exemplified by the various machine models produced by NordicTrack since 1976, may soon rank as America's number-one exercise choice. In the first place, it can burn more calories in less time than any other form of exercise, up to 1,100 calories per hour. At the same time, it is a total body workout, training all major muscle groups in both the upper and the lower body. Finally, there is no jarring or pounding that could harm your back.

Be warned that some skill is involved; it is not as easy as it looks in the TV ads. One of my most tenacious patients, Amanda R., had a particularly tough time at first. When her husband brought a NordicTrack home, set it up in the basement, and began to exercise with obvious zest and enjoyment, she was eager to try. Unlike him, however, she had not grown up in a rural wintry climate where cross-country skiing had been as natural and common as walking is to a city dweller. For four weeks, she kept coming to my office for treatment for bumps, scrapes, and even a sprained ankle, because she kept falling off the thing. When she finally learned how to coordinate her movements, though, she was on the Curve within only two weeks.

Few exercisers have quite that much difficulty with NordicTrack, but you have to pay special attention to keeping your balance while standing erect, with elbows straight, and remembering to put your entire weight on the forward foot as you push it backward in a smooth, gliding motion. The manufacturer supplies clear, complete instructions for using the machine properly, and you would be wise to read them carefully.

Skating is less physically demanding and aerobically rewarding, although it does require practice and skill. I think it's wonderful as an adjunct to complement any exercise program. As in swimming, you have to resist the temptation to glide blithely around the rink or over the secluded frozen pond, forgetting that you are in the business of maintaining your target heart range.

Ice skating and roller skating now have been combined in *rollerblading* or *in-line skating*. Using high-tech skates that feature a molded plastic boot and a single row of four or five polyurethane disks as wheels, you can easily achieve speeds near 30 miles per hour on any city street or sidewalk—and that's one of the chief disadvantages. Injuries from falls, bumps, scrapes, and crashes are common, and the skater who tries to prevent a collision or spill may shatter his wrist. Rollerbladers with a grim sense of humor use the term "road rash" to describe the condition of your skin after a bad spill.

Still, the sport is one of the three fastest-growing in the country, and its supporters are becoming increasingly safety-conscious. They are attracted not only by the speed and convenience but by the strenuous aerobic lower-body workout, which is equivalent to running without the jolts to the body (as long as you don't fall). And, as one skater has noted, "[Rollerblading] gives you freedom and mobility . . . peace of mind almost."

Skiing and Skating on the Curve

As with swimming, skiing and skating have a pitfall: when you are simply gliding across the snow or sliding over the ice, you are not doing the exercise work necessary for maintaining your target heart range. (Downhill skiing cannot be used on the Curve.)

In cross-country skiing, whether on ski trails or on an exercise machine, and in skating, you have to work yourself up gradually to a complete exercise schedule if you are new to regular exercise. As you develop your skills and stamina, you should be practicing how to take your pulse while you exercise, consistently working on your mood cards and faithfully making notes in your exercise diary. Within the first few sessions, your mood should be at level zero. Your eventual goal, which may take as long as a month to reach if you are not in shape, is to be able to work at target heart range for three 20-minute sessions each week. At that point, you move into Phase II.

As I explained in Chapter Nine, Phase II is a time for enjoyment. It helps to begin your work by finding music with a beat that is equivalent to the pace you now find comfortable. With every week, you should be more fully aware of the benefits of the Curve: elevated mood, improved stamina, a growing sense of all-around physical well-being. Along with the fun, however, you must take care that your pace is correct. When you ski or skate too quickly or too slowly for your personal level of fitness, your mood levels will begin to drop. A bad mood is a warning that you may be working at the wrong pace.

In Phase III, your skill at finding the correct pace is, of course, essential. In this phase, the goal is to fine-tune your exercise program, playing around with one factor at a time in order to sustain optimum mood levels. When you make a change, either in pace or in a resistance setting on the Nordic-Track, stick with it for at least a week in order to assess the effect of the change correctly.

Stair Climbing, Stair Master

In New York, where I live, extremely fit people who work out strenuously at their health clubs three times a week are outraged when the elevators go out and they have to consider climbing a few flights of stairs. That's only human. They didn't pay $150 a month in club membership fees and buy designer sweatsuits to climb their own stairs. Perhaps if the super affixed a sign to the stairwell reading "Aerobic Ascender" . . .

In fact, stair climbing as a form of regular aerobic exercise is now, according to *American Sports Data*, the fastest growing in the United States, attracting a diversity of adherents from George Bush to Jesse Jackson. The main reason is the development of remarkable machines (e.g., the Stair Master) that accurately monitor heart rate, workout pace, calories burned, number of floors climbed—a whole encyclopedia of vital statistics. Some give the sensation of climbing stairs; others make you feel as if you're standing up riding a stationary bicycle. The most complex machines can be quite expensive, but regulars believe that working on them burns about 10 percent more calories per hour than pedaling stationary bicycles. In addition, you work the entire lower body, from hips to calves, as well as the abdominal and lower back muscles. If the machine has handgrips for pulling, you simultaneously exercise your arms and chest, burning even more calories. The machines can be bad for you if you have runner's knee or a lower back problem; those conditions will get worse.

Stair-climbing machines can be steady-state or simulate climbing a hill. Despite any temptation you might feel to try the challenges of the hill-climbing type, for the purposes of the Curve you should stay with the steady-state machines. (When you are appropriately trained, you can use the hill-climbing type in interval training, the exercise routine I explain in the next chapter.) Naturally, the Stair Master has the advantage that you can watch TV while you're working out, and it takes up very little space. All in all, this device offers a very good workout. Still, the cost-conscious can take heart from Steve Farrell, of the Institute for Aerobic Research in Dallas: "There is nothing magical about the machines. You can get the exact same benefit from just climbing stairs in the home or office."

In fact, there are advantages to actual stairwells, according to Steve Silva, director of fitness programming at Health Management Resources in Boston. "At home or at work you're never far away from stairs," he points out. "They're in a controlled environment, no weather problems. You soon learn to develop a smooth motion that avoids the kind of pounding you get when you run. I've not been injured in more than nine years of climbing."

You burn extra calories when stair climbing because you are moving your body vertically as well as horizontally, as in walking or running. On the average flight of stairs (15 steps) the number of calories you burn is equal to your weight divided by 50. While providing an enormously strenuous workout that can be even more rigorous than a run taking the same amount of time, a session of stair climbing avoids the kind of impact upon bones and joints that can occur in running. At the same time, you can easily monitor and control your progress in this activity. At each step on a stair-climbing device, you can adjust your pace and resistance on the machine to suit your individual program. Stair climbing could exacerbate problems associated with weak front-thigh muscles, unstable knees, lower back pain, or ankle problems. People with these conditions should approach this form of exercise with caution. On the other hand, careful exercisers with injuries from other sports can use stair climbing successfully because the activity does not jolt the joints.

Does stair climbing sound dull? For some people, it provides so much pleasure (apparently, as much as swimming provides to me) that it becomes something close to an obsession. You can't get them off the machines.

And they love to come up with events like the annual "Empire State Run Up" sponsored by the New York Road Runners Club, in which competitors race up 86 flights of stairs (1,860 steps) to the top of the building that was once famous as the world's tallest. Similar competitions have sprung up around the world. (For comparison, the Eiffel Tower has 1,652 steps, the Gateway Arch in St. Louis has 1,076 steps, the Washington Monument has 898 steps, and the Space Needle in Seattle has 832 steps. For most of us, a moderate 15-minute workout in stair-climbing will include about 1,300 steps.)

Crazy? Well something is working for these stair climbers, and the results in increased aerobic capacity are spectacular. According to one study, men who climbed six flights or more daily suffered 25 percent fewer heart attacks than men who didn't climb at all. Stair climbing is worth serious consideration as you plan your exercise because of the results as well as the intrinsic convenience.

Stair Climbing on the Curve

Like stepping or running, stair climbing or using the Stairmaster may surprise the beginning exerciser by presenting unexpected difficulties, if you press too hard. Don't climb to the point of exhaustion. Climb at a rate that is slightly challenging but comfortable. Even experienced exercisers, used to another form of exercise, might not be ready to start working at target heart range for 20-minute sessions right away. For the first week, beginners should not worry about achieving target heart range. Whatever your level of fitness, let your body tell you when to stop as you develop your program. Ten-minute sessions may be the best way to start; then add 2 minutes or so to your workout each week, gradually building up to 20 minutes.

In Phase I, you need to practice the essentials: taking your pulse before, during, and after the workout, making the appropriate notations in your exercise diary, doing the mood cards so that you accurately track your mood levels. In Phase I, you are trying to reach mood level zero and maintain it.

Phase II begins when you are comfortably working at target heart range for 20 minutes three times a week. You have found a pace of climbing that works for you as an individual; now you should try to find a song that matches that pace, so you can work toward Phase III. (Some of my patients use music in Phase I. That's all right with me; I don't have a hard-and-fast rule.) If you are feeling slightly "down" after a session of climbing, something is probably wrong with your pace. You have slipped back into Phase I. Adjust your pace upward or downward until your mood elevates again. After all, the prevailing feeling of Phase II should be joy: the joy of discovering how much fun regular exercise can be, the joy of seeing the first wonderful benefits of aerobic exercise actually affecting your daily life.

When you move into Phase III, your mood should be sustained at the optimum level. Keeping it there will require fine-tuning your climbing pace. By this point, the mood cards, the pulse taking, and the diary notations should be routine. You are on Maharam's Curve. Just remember that fine-tuning will be required again when your fitness level rises so that your pace is no longer challenging enough to keep you on the Curve. In Phase III you learn and affirm the techniques that you will be using for the rest of your life.

Cross Training

If "Bo knows," so does the successful and personable boxer Ray "Boom Boom" Mancini, who built himself into a formidable fighting machine with a well-rounded combination of fitness activities that both honed skills and created a wholly fit body. When I asked Boom Boom to suggest tips for helping the nonathlete enjoy regular exercise, he deftly summed up the whole concept of cross training: "Always remember, you only get out of something what you put in. To cross train, do a series of different types of workouts to keep it fresh and not go stale."

Joe Morris, the New York Giants running back, said something very similar: "Do something different every week. Do not lock into one set pattern. Use your whole body."

For professional athletes like these two men, their challenge in the off-season is to keep the physical and mental edge they need to succeed in their demanding jobs. If they take time to work on the muscles and other body parts that aren't subjected to primary stress during their sport's season, they find that their overall strength and coordination are enhanced. When they return to the playing field in the new season, their performance will be dramatically improved by this cross training. In addition to the obvious physical benefits, however, the variety afforded by cross training provides the psychological benefit of a fresh perspective to the overworked pro. The epitome of the concept of cross training is the Ironman World Triathlon Championship—a marathon race, plus a 2.4-mile swim, plus a 112-mile bicycle race. It has helped encourage exercisers to vary their workouts by combining cycling or swimming with their regular running programs.

You will eventually find that you need a similar type of change, once you've become acclimated to a specific exercise routine and have gained strength and confidence in your understanding of your body's continuing development. Before you get into a rut, you should look for variety. Avoid predictability and burnout by taking up a new kind of exercise for a session or two, in addition to your regular exercise program. The simplest variation—swimming Mondays and Fridays, walking Wednesdays and Sundays—will bring excitement back into your exercise schedule.

For someone having difficulty moving out of Phase I, for example, variety in exercise can change the mindset just that crucial amount—and bring on Phase II.

In general, however, you should not try to substitute cross training for a single exercise when you are trying to maintain and fine-tune your Curve. Consider how much control would be needed to keep your diary notations accurate. If you set up a schedule that includes two forms of exercise, you also have to find the proper pacing in each. Any change in pace in one type of exercise is going to require a commensurate change in the other exercise. But how do you translate from one sport to another? There is no easy way.

On Maharam's Curve, cross training becomes incredibly complex. I've tried it with a couple of patients, at their insistence, but we were soon at wit's end, trying to compare apples and oranges. Since cross training is certainly healthy for mind and body, and I like it myself, I suggest that my clients *add* it to the Curve. In other words, stick to one exercise three times a week for the Curve; add a different activity for fun.

Weights and Circuit Training

Weight training, no longer considered solely a man's activity, is popular because of the positive effect upon looks and strength, but it can also give you an efficient aerobic workout. Supermodel Laura Ballard describes the attraction that many feel: "I wanted to get involved with a more personalized training program, something that would allow me to work on specific areas of my body—building in one place, reducing in another, shaping up where necessary."

Balancing that attraction, however, is the fairly common fear that weight training will increase strength at the expense of coordination and flexibility. Actually, this activity, if properly performed, will improve flexibility, because the muscles are stretched in full-length, range-of-motion strength training. Coordination is not hampered and may even be slightly enhanced. In addition, you can increase your speed, because the training involves the white, fast-twitch fibers in your muscles that govern speed as well as strength. Endurance is improved because of the training of the red, slow-twitch fibers in the muscles.

Less well known are the benefits of weight training to the inner workings of your body. We now know that moderate weight lifting can help lower blood pressure and cholesterol as well as blood-sugar levels, promote weight loss, improve your sex life, and help prevent knee, shoulder, and back injuries. These benefits come primarily from doing many repetitions with medium weights (say, one-half the maximum weight you can lift), without much rest between each set.

To avoid problems, you should begin slowly with no more than one half-hour workout every other day, with light weights of no more than 5 to 10 pounds. For exercising at home, you need only purchase a pair of dumbbells, a barbell, and several different types of interchangeable weights. As with all other strenuous forms of exercise, you should consult your physician before beginning a program, and you should find an expert coach or trainer to help you plan your workouts. It is essential to learn proper technique. The principal advantage of a gym program over home workouts is that an expert can help you monitor your progress and correct any developing bad habits.

For runners who want to increase their strength, a weight-training program can be effective if you work out with weights at least twice a week, run easily on the days you use weights so that you are rested before doing the weight training, avoid stress on the lower back by doing most lifting in the seated or lying-down position, and reduce risk of injury by concentrating on high repetitions with light weights.

For athletes who are highly competitive, there seems to be a slight advantage in training first for strength and then for endurance in your daily workout. For beginners in the sport, the best news is that results are evident quite rapidly. "The average person," says Peter Lemon, Ph.D., a professor of exercise physiology at Kent State University, "will realize tremendous improvements because most of us are sorely unfit from a strength standpoint."

To gain greater strength and muscular endurance as well as the cardiovascular benefits of aerobic exercise, serious exercisers sometimes turn to *circuit training*. Essentially, you set up a series of 10 to 15 exercises in a row or circle around a room and work the circuit two or three times. Each of the exercises is performed at lower than usual intensity; in most programs, the exerciser rests 30 seconds between each exercise. It is possible, for example, to do a 10-exercise circuit three times in one half-hour.

There are many different variations. Experienced weight trainers will choose the one that best suits their individual aims. Recently, some exercisers have added aerobic dance or an aerobic activity like cycling or treadmill work to their circuits. Others will use the circuit-training approach in the especially intense exercise known as interval training, which is explained in the next chapter.

Weight Training on the Curve

For the Curve, pace is still the most important variable in weight training, as in other forms of exercise. At first glance, it might seem to some that changing the weights would adjust you properly on the Curve, but that is inaccurate.

The weight-training pathway to the Curve is not recommended for the beginning exerciser, because it requires instruction, oversight, and practice. For the experienced weightlifter, experimentation will be necessary to find the comfortable amount of weight that you can lift at a steady, slow pace for the 20 minutes at target heart range that is essential to getting on the Curve. Even if you are an experienced lifter, this new approach may take a while. If you cannot lift steadily in target heart range for 20 minutes, stop when you feel discomfort and use that session as your baseline, working up to lengthier sessions gradually over the next few weeks. Phase I ends, as I explained in Chapter Eight, when you are able to lift weights at your individual pace and stay in target heart range for three 20-minute sessions each week.

In Phase I, you begin by working up to mood level zero and learning to sustain that feeling. Remember to get into the important habit of taking notes for your exercise diary. Practice taking your pulse before, during, and after your work-out. Become so familiar with the mood cards that flipping through them takes mere seconds. (You will have to find an exercise club that is unusually quiet or work at home as you learn and practice the rudiments of life on the Curve.)

When you're ready for Phase II, or even before, find a song that matches the pace you've been using in your lifting. During this phase, when every session should be a pleasure and life outside the exercise room should be improved physically and mentally, your principal assignment is to enjoy, to experiment, and to listen to your body. If you work too hard or slow down from your correct exercise pace, your mood levels will begin to drop. With that first warning sign, you should begin to adjust your pace.

By Phase III, you should be consistently at the optimum mood level. This is the period of fine-tuning your pace, of adjusting your workout until you find the routine that will work for the next few weeks or months—until your level of fitness rises so much that you have to adjust your pace again. No matter how well things go, remember that you cannot begin slacking off on the essentials of assessing your work: pulse, diary, mood cards. You'll feel great, but don't let that great feeling distract you from the routine that got you there!

Choose It

Any of the activities I've described, and many others, will help you find your way to exercise enjoyment on Maharam's Curve, so long as you remember that you have to attain a base level of fit muscles and a healthy heart.

Choose well.
Go slowly.
Follow my advice.
Do the mood cards.
Trust your body.

Trust your mind.

You will learn the truth behind Maharam's Curve: the right approach to exercise of mind and body in sync with each other will provide predictable physical and mental pleasure for the rest of your life.

That's it.

CHAPTER FOURTEEN

THE FINISH

When you are fit and feeling good, don't worry, like Alexander the Great, that there are no more worlds to conquer. I suggest you try the extraordinary challenge offered by *interval training*.

The basic idea of interval training is to push your body to its anaerobic threshold, where it stops getting most of its energy from oxygen and draws upon other sources. Why? Because interval training will teach your body to use those sources with greater efficiency, and because it will help you postpone the point at which you have to rely upon them. In your aerobic exercise pace, whatever your sport, you push your heart rate to between 70 and 85 percent of its maximum. For interval training, you *briefly* push the rate above 85 percent.

"Why ignore your anaerobic energy systems?" asks Dr. Craig Cisar, an exercise physiologist at San Jose State University in California. "If you view fitness as multidimensional, you wouldn't ignore muscle strength and endurance, flexibility or nutrition." By overloading the body's two metabolic systems that are anaerobic (lactic acid system, ATP-

PC system), interval training improves your cardiovascular endurance and your aerobic capacity. The body is trained to stay inside its aerobic comfort zone while pumping more blood and working harder.

But this type of exercise has to be carefully planned. If you are cycling, for example, you begin a session of interval training by working up to your maximum heart rate in 5 or 10 minutes. Next you raise your heart rate to 85 to 90 percent for 2 minutes. Then you slow down to your usual pace for 4 minutes, or until your heart rate drops to 70 percent. You repeat this sequence four to six times. After this strenuous workout, slow down, below your regular pace, until your heart rate drops to 60 percent. Then repeat the previous alternating sequence another four to six times, and finish off your interval training session by pedaling slowly at 60 percent heart rate for 5 to 10 minutes.

Similar interval-training programs for other sports are available in sports magazines. All incorporate relatively short periods of maximum activity or sprinting, because the body needs to recover after such stress in order to avoid fatigue and to speed the breakdown of lactic acid produced by your muscles during the sprint. Recovery comes more quickly with diminished activity, such as the slower pedaling, than with complete rest. After an interval of 1 to 3 minutes, recovery should be twice as long. Intervals of 3 to 5 minutes require the same amount of time for recovery. If your resting heart rate between workouts is 15 to 20 beats higher than normal, your body is not recovering sufficiently.

For runners, interval training builds up speed during the high-intensity intervals. For greater endurance, runners lower the intensity of the intervals but do more of them. When you use interval training, you should vary the intensity of your workouts. (Note: your "maximum effort" is the speed you achieve at a specific distance during an all-out run.) In order to keep these varying sessions roughly equal in quality, the following table is useful. It explains how many repetitions of an interval at one level of intensity are required in order to duplicate the effort of another level of intensity. For example, if you were to run 16 intervals at 80 percent of maximum effort, the equivalent would be 2 intervals at 90 percent effort.

DETERMINING EQUIVALENT WORKOUTS

PERCENTAGE OF MAXIMUM EFFORT	REPETITION	REST IN MINUTES
90	1	4–5
85	4	3–4
80	8	2–3
75	14	1–2
70	20	1–1.5

The results of properly executed interval training can be dramatic. In a 12-week study at the University of Miami's Human Performance Lab, college-aged women were divided into two groups: one did aerobic dance without a break for 35 minutes three times a week; the other exercised for a slightly longer period, aerobic dancing for 3- to 5-minute intervals and then resting by walking briskly in between each interval. In both groups, the exercisers trained for the entire session in the 75 percent to 85 percent target heart range. At the end of the experiment, exercise physiologist Dr. Arlette Perry found that the women who only danced aerobically showed an 8 percent improvement in cardiovascular endurance. The women who did interval training improved by 18 percent.

Obviously, this type of training is appropriate only to the most fit exercisers. Unless your physician agrees, you should never go above 90 percent of your maximum heart rate.

I have one more set of guidelines to discuss. As a sports physician, I find myself unable to resist stressing a very important warning, in addition to my earlier advice on proper preparation: prepare, prepare, and yet again prepare.

Before Exercising: Maharam's "Safe Seven"

To supplement Dr. Levy's five-point warm-up, warm-down program, I've devised a checklist of my "Safe Seven" pre-exercise tips, pneumonically arranged as "STRETCH." These tips are primarily written for beginners, but, no matter how long you've been running or engaging in other forms of exercise on a regular basis, you should glance down this list. These are tips you should always follow; you will never outgrow them or develop beyond them. If you're just starting out, you will need to think about each tip.

MAHARAM'S SAFE SEVEN

S: Stretch before and after any exercise workout.
T: Take it slow. Beginners shouldn't try to run a marathon the first day.
R: Rehearse. Before you exercise, take about 5 minutes to visualize what you want to accomplish.
E: Evaluate. Before you start your program, you should have a physical examination with your family physician or a specialist in sports medicine. This professional evaluation will help ensure that your exercise program is going to be helpful to you as well as safe.
T: Table manners. Drink plenty of water. Never eat a large meal before exercising. (Good nutrition is important, as I explained in detail in Chapter Five.)
C: Choose carefully. That applies to everything—the cor-

rect type of exercise, the correct athletic shoes or sneakers, the correct weight of clothing for the climate where you exercise.

H: Heart rate. Remember, it is critically important to cal- culate the estimated maximum heart rate range as- sociated with your exercise program.

From my point of view, of course, tip E for Evaluate is perhaps the most important. In some cases, a patient is dis- tressed because a minor injury or physical malfunction has made regular exercise painful or seemingly impossible. By the same token, a beginner is hardly going to respond to the benefits of Maharam's Curve by trying to exercise while ig- noring a medical problem. As I discussed in Chapter Four, exercise can be inefficient, unproductive, or even dangerous if you are not aware of actual or potential physical problems.

The Long Haul

Patience is more than a virtue in exercise; it may be the key to keeping yourself fit for the rest of your life. According to James Rippe, M.D., associate professor of medicine and di- rector of the Exercise Physiology and Nutrition Lab at the University of Massachusetts Medical School, the person who has the best chance of making exercise a lifelong habit is the one who "breaks the six-month barrier." Before then, you may experience periods of doubt and fatigue, and you may become distracted by unexpected events in your per- sonal or professional life. Or, like a very few of my patients, you may become so pleased with your success on Maha- ram's Curve that you become overconfident, stop keeping track of your mood levels, and suddenly find that exercise is a chore again.

Keep at It

As I promised in the beginning, Maharam's Curve really can change your life by making workouts so enjoyable that you will continue to work for the benefits of exercise. Consider the many different advantages of fitness we have discussed throughout this book. Longer life. Better sex. Leaner, more supple, more attractive bodies. Greater strength and endurance. Resistance to disease. Cure of mild depression.

Yet, as we all know, that list is not enough to convince four out of five Americans to continue exercising properly, simply because exercise has been slandered by the gain-through-pain school of working out.

With the Curve, the problem is solved.

You'll work hard but you won't suffer, because the mood scale combined with your diary records will help you learn to enjoy your workouts and look forward to the next session. You'll earn the many benefits of exercise and add another: the balance that includes mind and body, diet and exercise, in one perfect circle of good health and mental well-being.

If you have an unusually fine experience, or if you encounter a problem, I hope you will take a few moments to sit down and write me. One of the problems of writing a book for a general audience is that I don't have the benefit of personally talking with each individual reader, of course, and cannot be certain that my advice is targeted precisely for any uncommon situation. Your letters will help me fine-tune the next edition of this book so that it will be more responsive to the many possibilities of the Curve. Perhaps there are special circumstances that I have not yet encountered in my sports medicine practice. If so, I am eager to learn about them and work on whatever challenge they present. Just write to Dr.

Lewis G. Maharam, c/o W.W. Norton & Company, 500 Fifth Avenue, New York, NY 10110.

Finally, at this point, if you've read through this book chapter by chapter and worked on the various aspects of exercise that form the circle of balance and equilibrium, Maharam's Curve is an integral part of your life.

Perhaps your friends and relatives are doing it too, and you all speak the language of the Curve, sharing this wonderful new adventure of linking mood with exercise.

But remember my previous warning: life on the Curve is so pleasurable that you may begin to slacken. If your mood levels start to drop, read Chapter Three again and pay special attention to the mood cards. And remember that you are using the Curve as a tool for keeping healthy. As you become fitter it will be harder to stay on the Curve, unless you remember that frequent adjustment of your pace is necessary to sustain optimum mood levels.

This prescription is easily followed, because the slightest indication of consistently lowering mood levels is a sign that you are beginning to slide off the Curve.

Put positively, as long as you work to stay on the Curve, your mood levels will remain high, you may even occasionally feel the "exercise explosion," you are certainly going to feel mentally, emotionally, and physically better with each day, and you will have a longer, sexier, more active, more creative life.

Enjoy the ride.

APPENDIX A:
THE BALANCED DIET

For breakfast, have at least one choice of each:
  Breads, cereals, grains
  Fruits, fruit juices
  Skim or one-percent-fat milk or other low-fat dairy products

For lunch and dinner, have at least one choice of each:
  Breads, cereals, grains
  Fruits, fruit juices
  Skim or one-percent-fat milk or other low-fat dairy products
  Vegetables
  Fish, poultry, or lean meats
  Fats or oils

For seconds and snacks, have your choice of the following:
  Vegetables
  Fruits, fruit juices
  Breads, cereals, grains
  Skim or one-percent-fat milk

Extra Points for Health and Maximum Performance

Breads, cereals and grains:
Choose plain, whole-grain products without added fat whenever possible.
Choose non-granola cereals without nuts and seeds that are low in fat and sugar.

Fruit and fruit juices:
Choose fresh, whole fruits whenever possible.
Buy fruit juices, preferably citrus juices or juices supplemented with Vitamin C, instead of juice drinks.

Dairy products:
Use skim or low-fat dairy products such as skim or 1-percent-fat milk or cottage cheese.
Other low-fat dairy products include nonfat or low-fat yogurt, egg whites or cholesterol-free egg substitutes, and reduced-fat/reduced-calorie cheeses.

Vegetables:
Choose brightly colored, fresh or frozen vegetables, preferably without added fat.

Fish, poultry and lean meats:
Choose fish, seafood, and poultry more often than beef and other red meats.
Have poultry without skin whenever possible.
Have fresh, nonbreaded, and nonfried fish whenever possible.

Fats and oils:
Use reduced-fat or "diet" margarine, mayonnaise, and salad dressings for less fat.
Use salad dressings without cream or cheese.
Use olive oil or canola oil instead of other oils whenever possible.

APPENDIX B: APPROXIMATE CALORIES USED PER HOUR

APPENDIX B: APPROXIMATE CALORIES USED PER HOUR

ACTIVITY	205-POUND PERSON	125-POUND PERSON
Archery	420	268
Baseball —infield or outfield	382	234
—pitching	488	299
Basketball—moderate	575	352
—vigorous	807	495
Bicycling —on level, 5.5 mph	409	251
13.0 mph	877	537
Canoeing—4 mph	565	352
Dancing —moderate	341	209
—vigorous	464	284
Fencing —moderate	409	251
—vigorous	837	513
Football	678	416
Golf —twosome	443	271
—foursome	332	203
Handball or hardball—vigorous	797	488

ACTIVITY	205-POUND PERSON	125-POUND PERSON
Horseback riding —walk	270	165
—trot	551	338
Motorcycling	297	182
Mountain Climbing	820	503
Rowing—pleasure	409	251
—rowing machine or sculling 20 strokes/min.	1116	684
Running—5.5 mph	887	537
—7 mph	1141	669
—9 mph level	1269	777
—9 mph 2.5% grade	1480	907
—9 mph 4% grade	1564	959
—12 mph	1606	984
—in place 140 count/min.	1993	1222
Skating —moderate	465	285
—vigorous	837	513
Skiing —downhill	789	483
—level, 5 mph	956	586
Soccer	730	447
Squash	849	520
Swimming—backstroke - 20 yds./min.	316	194
- 40 yds./min.	682	418
—breaststroke - 20 yds./min.	392	241
- 40 yds./min.	786	482
—butterfly	956	586
—crawl - 20 yds./min.	392	241
- 50 yds./min.	869	532
—sidestroke	682	418
Tennis —moderate	565	347
—vigorous	797	488
Volleyball—moderate	465	285
—vigorous	797	489
Walking —2 mi./hr.	286	176
—110–120 paces/min.	425	260

ACTIVITY	205-POUND PERSON	125-POUND PERSON
—4.5 mph	540	331
—downstairs	544	333
—upstairs	1417	869
Water Skiing	638	391
Wrestling, Judo or Karate	1049	643

Reprinted with permission from *Nutrition for Sport Success,* © 1984, American Alliance for Heath, Physical Education, Recreation and Dance.

APPENDIX C: IMPORTANT ADDRESSES FOR RIDERS OF THE CURVE

American Dietetic Association
208 S. LaSalle
Chicago, IL 60604-1003
Tel. (800) 621-6469

American Running and Fitness Association
9310 Old Georgetown Rd.
Bethesda, MD 20814
Tel. (800) 776-ARFA

Gabriele Andersen's Swiss Alpine Marathon Training Week
4686 Mossy Lane
Lilburn, Atlanta, GA 30247

Central Park Track Club
7 W. 96th St.
New York, NY 10025

Clydesdale Runners Association
1809 Gold Mine Rd.
Brookeville, MD 20833

Craftsbury Running Camp
PO Box 31-B
Craftsbury Common, VT 05827

Dartmouth College Camp
Contact: John Holland
2434 Hawthorne Dr.
Yorktown Heights, NY 10598

Florida Runners Camp
1447 Peachtree St., Suite 804
Atlanta, GA 30309

Foss Running Camp
RFD #1, Box 217
Barnstead, NH 03218

Gold Medal Camp
48 Morris St.
Clymer, PA 15728

Green Mountain Running Camp
Contact: John Holland
2434 Hawthorne Dr.
Yorktown Heights, NY 10598

Metropolitan Racewalkers
36 W. 20th St.
New York, NY 10011

New England Running Camp
P.O. Box 359
Scituate, MA 02066

Newport Running Camp
Ted Hersey
Saint George's School
Newport, RI 02840

New York Cycle Club
P.O. Box 199, Cooper Station
New York, NY 10276

New York Road Runners Club Fitness Vacations
Contact: Beryl Bender
NYRRC
9 E. 89th St.
New York, NY 10128

Team Redline (Triathlon)
365 W. 52nd St.
New York, NY 10019

Walkers Club
Howard Jacobson, Box M
Livingston Manor, NY 12758
(send self-addressed, stamped, legal-size envelope)

Walkers Club of America
445 E. 86th St.
New York, NY 10028
(send SASE)

APPENDIX D:
STRETCHING EXERCISES

5 times
each direction

20 seconds

3

shoulder blade pinch
2 times
5 seconds each

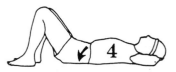

flatten lower back
2 times
5 seconds each

SOURCE: Excerpted from *Stretching* © 1980 by Bob and Jean Anderson. $9.95 Shelter Publications, Inc., P.O. Box 279, Bolinas, CA 94924. Distributed in book stores by Random House. Reprinted by permission.

3 times
5 seconds each

20 seconds
each side

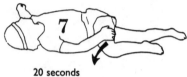

20 seconds
each side

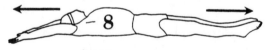

2 times
5 seconds each

20 seconds
each leg

30 seconds

10 seconds
each side

30 seconds
each leg

20 seconds
each leg

10 times
each direction

30 seconds
each foot

15 seconds
each leg

20 seconds
each leg

25 seconds
each leg

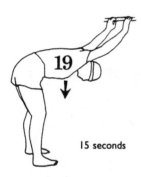

15 seconds

10 seconds
each arm

10 seconds

2–3 minutes

INDEX